Praise for *Whe*

"Dominic Done addresses the topic of doubt from a profoundly intellectual perspective but wraps it in his life story—a narrative about the challenges to his faith. Oxford educated, he knows the questions of the mind. As a pastor, he knows the burdens of the heart. As I read, Dominic captured both dimensions for me, and he will for you too. Doubt is such a pertinent issue in this cultural moment. Dominic walks us through the issues of doubt with which we wrestle but he does so in pastoral practicality. One feels as though you are seated in his living room sipping coffee. Dominic is the type of soul who understands the questions of the heart. He never shames. He's always transparent. He gives substantive hope. You will find yourself trusting him as he shepherds you on three important elements: relationship, intimacy, and trust. I do not doubt you will love this book!"

—EMERSON EGGERICHS, PhD, *NEW YORK TIMES* BESTSELLING AUTHOR OF *LOVE & RESPECT*

"This book is one of those books that I will be buying to give to multiple friends. It answers and encourages so brilliantly the questions many of us have and wrestle with in regard to doubt. I'm thankful for Dominic sharing his story, wisdom, and hard-fought truths with us and the rest of the world!"

—JEFFERSON BETHKE, *NEW YORK TIMES* BESTSELLING AUTHOR OF *JESUS > RELIGION.*

"*When Faith Fails* is a good reminder that we are all vulnerable and our faith fails easily because we look for quick answers on our time line, forgetting God has his own timing. I want to encourage people to read this book, especially if they have doubts and questions that can only be answered by God."

—SISTER ROSEMARY NYIRUMBE, DIRECTOR OF SAINT MONICA GIRLS' TAILORING CENTRE IN GULU, UGANDA, NOMINEE FOR A NOBEL PEACE PRIZE, AND ONE OF *TIME*'S 100 MOST INFLUENTIAL PEOPLE OF 2014

"So many people of faith are afraid and ashamed of doubt. I'm thankful that in this book, Dominic gives us permission to wrestle with God and life's hardest questions. He encourages us to walk through our doubt in order to find a deeper and richer faith on the other side."

—PHIL WICKHAM, SINGER, SONGWRITER

"Dominic helps us not to feel afraid of our finitude, ashamed of our doubt, or alone with our questions. This book is intelligent, well-written, and will be a real help to those going through the mill of doubt—and those who seek to support them."

—MICHAEL LLOYD, PRINCIPAL OF WYCLIFFE HALL, UNIVERSITY OF OXFORD

"This is the best book on doubt I've ever read. Dominic is a trustworthy guide, who's walked this haunting valley of doubt's shadow himself, and emerged with wisdom, insight—and humorous wit—on how to traverse its trail. *When Faith Fails* reveals that doubt is not the opposite or enemy of faith, but rather an opportunity to enter more deeply into God's faithfulness to us."

—JOSHUA RYAN BUTLER, PASTOR OF REDEMPTION CHURCH, PHOENIX, ARIZONA, AND AUTHOR OF *THE SKELETONS IN GOD'S CLOSET* AND *THE PURSUING GOD*

"Doubt can be a dark enemy that leaves faith in shambles or the catalyst to a deeper, better founded, more contagious faith. We must deal with these doubts whether they are intellectual, emotional, or social lest they move us to despair or denial. *When Faith Fails* is Dominic Done's personal story of his journey through doubt. He teaches us with his own responses to critical questions. He exemplifies the attitudes and tools for wrestling with our own haunting questions. It is a rare book, one that is both an intriguing biography and solid equipping."

—GERRY BRESHEARS, PhD, PROFESSOR OF THEOLOGY, WESTERN SEMINARY, PORTLAND

"As someone who has always been a challenger and likes asking hard questions, Dominic's book is a refreshing take on how doubting can be an opportunity for authentic vibrant faith. This book made me feel so much less alone in some of the hard questions I've wrestled with, and it's given me permission to keep wrestling with what I think, what I feel, and what Scripture says. As Dom puts it, 'doubt is not where faith ends, but where trust begins.' This book will help you surrender and trust the areas of your life that are meant to exude God-designed mystery, while also holding your hand as you search for substance and truth. This book is for anyone who wants to discover more of God and live a life of unshakable faith."

—AUDREY ROLOFF, FOUNDER OF ALWAYS MORE, COFOUNDER OF BEATING50PERCENT, AND COAUTHOR OF *A LOVE LETTER LIFE*

"Dominic hit the nail on the head in this amazing read. This is a book that all should gravitate to. We all—even believers—have seasons in life where our faith dwindles but this book is a reminder that we are not walking alone. If we just continue to tap into God's glorious power, he will lift us up in due time!"

—BRANDIN COOKS, WIDE RECEIVER FOR THE LOS ANGELES RAMS

"Dominic Done has taken a deep and personal dive into the difficult questions that haunt Christians the most. In a time when many people view skepticism as a threat to our faith, Done reframes the entire conversation. What if our doubts can become a gateway into new and deeper experiences of faith? Prepare to be challenged and encouraged, all at the same time!"

—TIM MACKIE, COCREATOR OF THE BIBLE PROJECT

"Doubt is an inevitable part of the Christian journey. Sadly, for many it can end up derailing their faith altogether. Combining personal experience, theological depth, and the heart of a pastor, Dominic Done has written an essential guide for navigating doubt. As the host of a religious radio debate show I am regularly contacted by people in the process of deconstructing their beliefs. I now know which book I will recommend to seekers, skeptics, and doubters who want to start putting their faith back together again. *When Faith Fails* is, quite simply, excellent."

—JUSTIN BRIERLEY, HOST OF THE UNBELIEVABLE? SHOW
AND AUTHOR OF *UNBELIEVABLE? WHY, AFTER TEN YEARS
OF TALKING TO ATHEISTS, I'M STILL A CHRISTIAN*

"I love this book! Dominic's exploration of doubt is not only timely and necessary, it is essential for this generation. Why? Because we live in a skeptical generation where doubt is real. But Jesus is even more real, and he desires to meet us in the midst of a life that can be confusing. I love that Dominic is strongly tethered to the scriptures while still being free to explore the edges of our experiences with doubt. This is a must-read and I plan on putting this book into the hands of as many people as possible."

—DANIEL FUSCO, LEAD PASTOR OF CROSSROADS COMMUNITY
CHURCH AND AUTHOR OF *UPWARD, INWARD, OUTWARD* AND *HONESTLY*

"Dominic Done has written one of the most helpful and intriguing books on the subject of Christian doubt that I have ever encountered. It is a fantastic mix of scriptural guidance, careful observation of the struggles of others, and rich personal narrative. The result is hope, help, and a healthy path for those who are merely touched by doubt, but also for those who are tormented by doubt. This is a book with a wonderful pastoral texture that will be of immense benefit for groups to read together in the church. This is a standout volume with tremendous promise to revive true faith in an increasingly dark and skeptical age."

—CRAIG J. HAZEN, PHD, FOUNDER AND DIRECTOR
OF THE CHRISTIAN APOLOGETICS PROGRAM AT BIOLA
UNIVERSITY AND AUTHOR OF *FEARLESS PRAYERV*

"In an age of social frustration, political polarization, and doubt about the future, *When Faith Fails* embraces all the challenges of the present and encourages you to embrace a genuine dialogue with God. Dominic Done's work is intellectually challenging and deeply meaningful. He took me on a journey that significantly enhanced my own relationship with God, and for that I am deeply grateful. Much like my own reading of Dallas Willard, Dominic's book made me consistently reflect on my own relationship with God and he made possible the deepening of my spirit."

—ROBIN BAKER, PRESIDENT OF GEORGE FOX UNIVERSITY

when

faith

fails

when

faith

fails

FINDING GOD IN THE
SHADOW OF DOUBT

DOMINIC DONE

NELSON
BOOKS

An Imprint of Thomas Nelson

Published in Nashville, Tennessee, by Nelson Books, an imprint of Thomas Nelson. Nelson Books and Thomas Nelson are registered trademarks of HarperCollins Christian Publishing, Inc.

Thomas Nelson titles may be purchased in bulk for educational, business, fund-raising, or sales promotional use. For information, please email SpecialMarkets@ThomasNelson.com.

Unless otherwise noted, Scripture quotations are taken from the Holy Bible, New International Version®, NIV®. Copyright © 1973, 1978, 1984, 2011 by Biblica, Inc.® Used by permission of Zondervan. All rights reserved worldwide. www.Zondervan.com. The "NIV" and "New International Version" are trademarks registered in the United States Patent and Trademark Office by Biblica, Inc.®

Scripture quotations marked CEB are from the Common English Bible. Copyright © 2011 Common English Bible.

Scripture quotations marked CEV are from the Contemporary English Version. Copyright © 1991, 1992, 1995 by American Bible Society. Used by permission.

Scripture quotations marked KJV are from the King James Version. Public domain.

Scripture quotations marked NKJV are from the New King James Version®. © 1982 by Thomas Nelson. Used by permission. All rights reserved.

Scripture quotations marked NLT are from the Holy Bible, New Living Translation. © 1996, 2004, 2007, 2013, 2015 by Tyndale House Foundation. Used by permission of Tyndale House Publishers, Inc., Carol Stream, Illinois 60188. All rights reserved.

Any internet addresses, phone numbers, or company or product information printed in this book are offered as a resource and are not intended in any way to be or to imply an endorsement by Thomas Nelson, nor does Thomas Nelson vouch for the existence, content, or services of these sites, phone numbers, companies, or products beyond the life of this book.

ISBN 978-1-4002-0777-0 (eBook)
ISBN 978-1-4002-0776-3 (TP)

Library of Congress Cataloging-in-Publication Data

Library of Congress Control Number: 2018957869

Printed in the United States of America

19 20 21 22 23   LSC   10 9 8 7 6 5 4 3 2 1

To the doubters.
To the wounded, restless ones.
To the disenchanted, marginalized, thirsty,
confused, and questioning.
To those whose faith has failed.
To those barely clinging on.
To those who believe but are homesick for more of God.
These pages, these words, these stories are for you.

I want to beg you, as much as I can, dear sir, to be patient toward all that is unresolved in your heart and to try to love the questions themselves like locked rooms and like books that are written in a very foreign tongue . . . . The point is, to live everything. Live the questions now. Perhaps you will then gradually, without noticing it, live along some distant day into the answer.

—RAINER MARIA RILKE,
LETTERS TO A YOUNG POET

Contents

CONTENTS

Foreword

I WAS NEVER VERY GOOD AT SPELLING when I was young. Lots of us aren't. Truth be told, I'm still not that great at it. I'm told it's a genetic thing. We would have spelling tests in elementary school each week and I'd stand next to the teacher with my hands in my pockets looking at my shoes. My teacher would announce the next word to be spelled and I would awkwardly squirm as I slowly sounded out the word while the teacher looked on. As I did, it felt like my mind had just thrown a whole box of scrabble letters on the floor and I was on my hands and knees looking for the ones that had been lost under the couch.

More often than not, just when I thought I had spelled a word correctly, the teacher would let me know I'd missed a silent "e" at the end. It was a seemingly impossible deficit to overcome. Words like *love, dove,* and *above* continued to be my undoing. They sounded like they should be spelled *lov, dov,* and *abov* to me.

It turns out that the biggest distinguishing factor between those who spell well and those who don't is whether they can actually *see* the words in their minds. The reason I got the spelling words wrong most of the time was that simple. I just couldn't see them in my head before I tried to spell them out loud. What I started to do in order to compensate for the tide of mistakes I continued to make was to start adding an "e" to the end of every word I was uncertain about.

A lot of us are just as uncertain about matters relating to our faith as I was about spelling my words. That's why Dominic wrote this book. We try our best to live out our faith, only to feel like we've messed it up again. The problem with our faith is the same as it was with my spelling—sometimes we just can't really see it. What we then try to do is compensate.

Some of us compensate by using big religious words in our conversations, or projecting a lot more certainty about our faith than we actually have. Others make a big deal out of the things they do to draw attention to what they say they believe. Some find shelter in having big opinions and positions which seem to dwarf the appearance of love and acceptance in their lives. Here's the problem—every time we do these things, it's like we've added a silent "e" to our faith.

God isn't an editor, he's a creator. He's not looking for the typos in our lives, he's looking for the beauty in them. He wants us to live authentically and bring him all of our questions. The reason is simple—he doesn't care what our faith looks like, he cares about what it is.

In the pages that follow, Dominic takes on some of the questions many of us have in our faith. This book is for those of us who have experienced a gut check, or two, when it comes to some of the intersections between our lives and our faith. It's for those of us who no longer want to add unnecessary explanations to our beliefs just because we can't fully see what God is doing in our lives. It's for people who want to stop adding a silent "e" to their faith.

In junior high I took a class on how to use a typewriter. I'm actually that old. There was no spell-check feature on these typewriters, just a lot of keys with letters and symbols on them. I wasn't very good at typing, but eventually I was able to pluck out a few words which included a pile of misspellings. My problem was the same. I kept adding an "e" at the end of most words—just in case.

There were actually more keys on typewriters back then than there are now. Let me explain. These days, if you write a friend and want to express some surprise, you would add a question mark followed by an exclamation mark. "You were kicked out of school? Really?!" When I was learning to type, there was actually an extra key which used to be on every typewriter, it was called an interabang. Get this—it's a question mark and an exclamation point put together as one symbol. Faith, to me, is a lot like an interabang. We all have questions about our faith. We're not sure why we should believe the Bible or the role of science in our faith or what to do when we can't hear God's voice. What Dom has done in this book is to put the exclamation mark after the important stuff on these questions and more.

We've all had difficult things happen to us. We've lost jobs or relationships or even loved ones. These are the times when the easy explanations—the kind you might find on a bumper sticker—don't work anymore. Dom has invited us in these pages to bring all of the questions we have to Jesus. He can handle them. In fact, this is what faith is. It's what we do with the questions we have. Paul said that faith is confidence in what we're hoping for, and assurance in what we haven't seen yet. That makes sense to me. Yet while I'm a pretty hopeful guy, hoping for great outcomes isn't what Paul was talking about. He was talking about God's ability to do infinitely more than we could ever imagine. Faith is about having confidence in what we're hoping for, even when we don't have certainty about how our lives will turn out.

Dominic doesn't tell you what to believe. Instead, he invites you and I to figure out where the question marks in our lives are and, instead of adding a silent "e" to our faith, to put an exclamation point after the things we can be certain of. He's a smart guy, but far more impressive to me is that Dominic is wise. He's not going to add an "e" to your faith. He'll just point you towards Jesus.

As you read through these pages, you're in for a treat. Let me introduce you to my friend, Dominic. You'll want to give some thought to what he has to say.

—Bob Goff, author of *Loves Does* and *Everybody, Always*

Introduction
When Faith Fails

I do believe; help me overcome my unbelief!
—Mark 9:24

CHANCES ARE YOU'RE READING this book because you or someone close to you is struggling with doubt. But it wasn't always that way. Your faith was once emphatically alive, soaked in wide-eyed wonder, joy-filled simplicity, and unflinching trust. It was everything. But then:

- You experienced a sudden loss—a friend, parent, or child. Your tattered heart screams, *Why?* But the answers you get feebly collapse in a flood of pain and grief. If faith can't help in times like this, then why have it?
- Perhaps your views have changed socially or politically, and that's reshaping how you understand the Bible. You used to love the Bible; it was your spiritual lifeline. But now you can't read it without noticing everything that offends you.
- Maybe you were hurt by the church or by someone you looked to as a spiritual mentor.

- You've immersed yourself in science, and now you're filled with piercing questions about its relationship to faith. Are the two compatible? You still want to believe, but you just don't think it makes sense anymore.
- Perhaps you've grown disillusioned because after years of prayer you've heard nothing. Your soul yearns for answers, but God remains silent.
- Or maybe you fell into the malaise of the commonplace. At one point, your faith in God animated and inspired everything in life. Your heart throbbed for him. But then you experienced what Eugene Peterson calls the "Badlands," the long, lonely stretches of mundane, boring living.[1] Your once-vibrant faith is now sedated by conference calls, diapers, exams, lawn mowers, Instagram notifications, office drama, and sitting in traffic.

Whatever the cause of your doubt—and that list alone could fill another book—you're here because you know that doubt is not only real but incredibly painful. And the pain is compounded because you don't know where to go or who to talk to. Who in your life will understand? Where can you go when the deepest part of you—your soul's intimacy with God—is being torn apart by uncertainty?

At this point, you're typically given two options—and neither one is good. One is to demonize your doubt: in this narrative, doubt is labeled as the nemesis of faith, and those who doubt are judged and marginalized. Friends may respond with a far-off, I-feel-sorry-for-you, have-you-read-your-Bible-lately look. Parents may get angry. Church leaders may misunderstand or criticize you.

The second option is to idolize your doubt. In the thrill of deconstruction and fueled by a growing genre of podcasts and books, you watch as your faith goes up in smoke. It feels so progressive to ridicule what you used to believe—and then you wake up one day to find you don't believe in anything anymore.

Both of these options leave us confused and unsettled. Neither one seems right. Where do we go from here?

I can't help but wonder if there is a third way, one that doesn't demonize or idolize doubt but recognizes doubt for what it is: an opportunity for authentic and vibrant faith.

That is why I wrote this book.

I wrote this book because you need to know that your doubts aren't a sign of spiritual collapse but of a faith that is screaming out for substance and truth.

I wrote this book because what you're longing for is not more scripted answers but a safe place where you can honestly wrestle with the questions.

I wrote this book because your doubt may be the best thing that has happened to you.

I wrote this book because God loves doubters. The Bible is full of them.

I wrote this book because God is with you in your doubt.

I wrote this book because I know what it feels like to doubt. I've been there.

I wrote this book because countless others have been there too. I want you to hear their stories. I want you to see them as they wrestle, agonize, and eventually encounter God.

And I want you to know that doubt isn't a destination but a road to be traveled.

» «

Of course, by definition, the subject of doubt is incredibly difficult to explore. In many ways, I feel like the mosquito in the nudist colony: I'm not sure where to begin! But if you're willing to invest the time to explore with me, here's how the journey will unfold.

In Part I, I'll start by thinking through the origin of doubt (chapter 1): Why is it such an enduring part of the human story? Why did God create the world this way? Then, we'll take a closer look at doubt (chapter 2), defining it and seeking to understand its place in our lives. In chapter 3, we'll see how disruptive seasons of doubt can be. Then, in chapter 4, I'll share some of my own story, how doubt has challenged and shaped my view of God.

In Part II, I'll move on to four specific issues that create doubt in our lives: Scripture (chapter 5), science (chapter 6), suffering (chapter 7), and the silence of God (chapter 8).

Finally, in Part III (chapters 9 through 11), I'll share vital and practical ways that we can grow through our doubts.

It is my hope that by the end of this book, you'll see that doubt is not how faith ends but how trust begins. Deep faith calls to us from the other side of agonizing doubt. Doubt can make your friendship with God more vulnerable, gritty, and alive. In fact, your doubt may be the very instrument that refines your faith so that only Jesus remains.

And even if your faith fails, he never will.

But I'm getting ahead of myself.

Before we get there, let's begin with doubt itself. Where does it come from, and is it normal? Why are there so many unanswered questions in life?

Part I

Far from Home:

How We Got Here

Chapter 1

Knowing We Don't Know

Below the surface, we do not know; we shall never
know why; we shall never know tomorrow . . .
this mysterious wall round our world and our
perception of it is not there to frustrate us but to
train us back to the now, to life, to our time being.
—JOHN FOWLES, *THE ARISTOS*

Blessed are the curious . . . for they
shall have adventures.
—LOVELLE DRACHMAN

THE FIRST STEP INTO something new often looks like trust, not clarity.

I began to discover the meaning of those words when I packed up everything I owned and moved from Oregon to the jungles of Vanuatu. Never heard of it? Neither had I when my pastor invited me to go. "It will be great," he said. "You'll be teaching a group of college-aged students who come from all over the country to learn." Impulsive, in my early twenties, and evidently ready for adventure, I said yes, then hurried to the store to pick up a map. I spent forty-five minutes searching for Vanuatu. Assuming it was in Africa, my eyes scoured the continent. Finally, I realized Vanuatu is nowhere near Africa. It's a group of eighty-two islands in the South Pacific, about 750 miles from Fiji. Still totally clueless, I said my goodbyes and got on a plane, about to begin one of the most exciting and unforgettable seasons of my life.

Weeks later, I sat around a fire with a group of new friends. "Dominic," my friend Vera asked, "tell us something about America. What's an area you love to visit?"

Several places immediately came to mind: the beach, Crater Lake, my favorite coffee shop I especially missed after months away. "I know," I said suddenly, "Disneyland!" The moment I said it, though, I felt a stab of regret. I was in *way* over my head.

Vanuatu is among the most primitive nations on earth. If you ever have the chance to visit, it's like stepping into an issue of *National Geographic*. We lived in huts. No electricity. No running water. I had to learn a new language called Bislama. Bislama is an English-based creole language that is extremely simple and descriptive. For example, the word *slingshot* (which they use for hunting) is *elastic blong shootem pijin*. The word *piano* is even more flamboyant. Rather than using the single word *piano*, you would say something like "Hemi wan box, wea got white teeth blong hem, mo got black teeth blong hem. Mo, suppose yu kilim teeth blong hem, hemi sing out long yu."

That's the word *piano*.

You can imagine the horror I felt when I was teaching theology and came across the word *propitiation*. And you can imagine the horror I was about to feel when asked about the Happiest Place on Earth.

"What's Disneyland?" a student asked.

"Well . . ." *Where do I even begin?* I wondered. So, I started with Mickey Mouse. "There's a giant mouse named Mickey, who lives in a part of America called California." The only problem was, there is no word for mouse in their language. The closest they had was the word *rat*. I started over. "There's a giant rat that lives in America . . . and he's big. Really big." (In Bislama, you say "big-fala.")

They nodded their heads. They had all seen their fair share of rodents of unusual size. Vanuatu was full of them.

"What's amazing about this rat," I continued, "is that he can talk."

Their eyes widened.

"Well, not really the rat . . . there's someone inside the rat."

They stared at me. "So . . . he eats people?" someone whispered.

"No, of course not. The person is alive. He makes the rat move."

"But . . . why?"

I was getting nowhere fast.

I switched gears and began telling them about the castle. But again, there is no word for castle in Bislama. The closest they had was *hut*.

"So . . ." I quickly continued, "there's a big-fala rat, and he lives inside a big-fala hut." I tried to describe the hut. The dimensions were bigger than anything they could envision. I could see the confusion etched on their faces. A hundred feet tall? Spires? The rat lives there? Why? And why would anyone want to visit? *What is this place?*

The confusion was rapidly growing. They murmured anxiously to one another.

I moved on to the teacups. "There are these big-fala cups!" I exclaimed. "You sit in them, and you spin around and around!"

They grew silent. At this point their minds were spinning like the cups.

Finally, one of them spoke up. It was Vera. "Dominic," he cautioned. "You must *never* go to Disneyland. It is an evil place."

The other students nodded passionately as he spoke.

"And Mickey," he continued. "Mickey is a witch doctor."

I laughed. They didn't. I changed the subject and asked them about fishing.

» «

I'll never forget that conversation around the fire.

There I was, relatively new to the Vanuatu culture. Trying to learn their language. Trying to eat their food (that's another story!). Trying to understand how they thought, what they believed, and how they did life. I knew so little. And what I clumsily explained was so foreign. So abstract. So bizarre.

I tried to put into words what I experienced to be real but quickly encountered the cultural chasm between us. There are some things that, unless you've been there and seen it yourself, cannot be brought to life with words alone. And this is true not only on an island in the South Pacific, sitting around a fire with a group of bewildered students. It's true of all of us, no matter where you live.

Our knowledge is opaque. Our perspective confined. We may deliberate, speculate, guess, and argue—but there are some things beyond our grasp.

To some, Disneyland is the Happiest Place on Earth. To others, it's controlled by an evil mastermind/witch doctor named Mickey.

» «

We live in a world of limitations.

There are limits, as I learned, to language, culture, and our view of the world. There are also limits to our intellect; no matter how much we read, research, or study, we still need Alexa or Siri to close the gaps. There are limits to our physical strength; even if we do CrossFit, yoga, and consume endless spinach smoothies, inevitably we'll come down with the flu. And there are limits to our lifetime. According to James 4:14, life is "a mist that appears for a little while and then vanishes." Snap your fingers and you're more raisin than grape. Life is short.

To be human is to encounter limitation in all its forms. There is so much we cannot do and so much we cannot know. Socrates admitted, "We do not know—neither the sophists, nor the orators, nor the artists, nor I—what the True, the Good, and the Beautiful is . . . I am strongly convinced that I am ignorant of what I do not know."[1] So not only do we live in a world of limits, but we are ignorant of what those limits are. We don't know what we don't know.

And to make matters worse, even those areas of life we are confident in are still prone to uncertainty. For example, I may believe that a friend genuinely loves me. I may even have evidence backing up that belief, but can I be 100 percent confident this is true? What if they're merely using me to get something they want? What if their "love" is a two-faced mask? Sometimes the most cherished beliefs we hold may turn out very different than we expected. Life is unpredictable.

The same can be said for science. In the domain of particle physics, scientists have a name for this. They call it the "Heisenberg Uncertainty Principle." This means that no matter how fine our instruments, it is difficult to predict an atom's position and momentum with absolute precision. It may appear in one location only to surprise you somewhere else. At the quantum level, things get even weirder. I recently had coffee with someone who has a background in physics (if you want to feel dumb, have coffee with a physicist!). He told me that not only can atoms take different paths than we expect, they can take different paths *at the same time*. In other words, even the most basic ingredients of existence—atoms—are defined by unpredictability.

Uncertainty lies at the heart of the universe.

How's that for a boost of confidence? It's not really. But track with me here, because this is leading somewhere, and it raises all kinds of interesting questions about the world and our place in it. At the top of that list is *why*? Why is the universe this way? Why are there so many barriers to our knowledge? Why would God make a world with so many unknowns?

Well, to help us understand, let's go to the book of Genesis, where it all began.

>> <<

The opening verses of the Bible begin with the radical assertion that God exists: "In the beginning God . . ." (Genesis 1:1).

But what kind of God is he? Theologians and philosophers have grappled with this question for millennia, and there is a dizzying array of ideas and perspectives. But where most agree is that God, by definition, possesses the following attributes: he is omniscient (all-knowing), omnipotent (all-powerful), omnipresent (everywhere at once), and eternal. In other words, he is a limitless God. Incalculable. Unrestricted. Nothing is beyond his grasp.

When my daughter was three, I once asked her, "What is God like?"

With a smile, she threw her arms out wide and gushed, "He is *sooo* big!" And in that answer, she basically summarized everything we could ever learn or read about God.

He is *big*. Beyond anything we could ever imagine. And at the dawn of all things, this big God created us.

Let that sink in.

An incomprehensibly infinite God created something. Like an artist standing before a canvas, he splashed boundless layers of color, life, beauty, fire, water, earth—and our world was born.

"And God saw that it was good" (Genesis 1:10).

Seven times in the creation story, God called his world good. He made the mountains, rivers, and seas and said, "It is good." He made the stars, planets, and the sun and said, "It is good." He made poetry, art, and pour-over coffee and said, "It is *very* good." The word *good* in Hebrew, the original language of the Old Testament, is בוט (pronounced "tove"). It means creation the way it was meant to be. Joy, beauty, virtue, flourishing, harmony—all are enveloped in this ancient understanding of goodness. When God spoke, the universe was vibrant and alive, humming with his presence.

But here's what's fascinating: the one word that isn't used to describe this new creation is *perfect*. That word doesn't show up until Genesis 6, and there it's used in a very different context. Why is this important? Because it means that from the very beginning, limitations were built into the system. It was good, but not perfect.

And maybe it *had* to be that way. After all, God, who is perfect, created the universe. But the universe is not God (pantheism), so when God created it, by definition, it was something less than God. The very act of creation was the initiation of limits. Look again at the first words of Genesis:

"In the beginning God created the heavens and the earth."

9

Here we see the basic ingredients of our universe: time (in the beginning), space (the heavens), and matter (the earth). In other words, an eternal God made a world limited by time. An immeasurable God made a world with the boundaries of space. An immaterial God made a world restricted by matter. Limitations were part of his design.

And he didn't stop there:

> Then God said, "Let us make mankind in our image, in our likeness, so that they may rule over the fish in the sea and the birds in the sky, over the livestock and all the wild animals, and over all the creatures that move along the ground." (Genesis 1:26)

God made the first humans. He began with Adam, then he created Eve. Someone once joked that God took one look at man, said, "I can do better than that," and then created woman! That's probably true, but whatever the reason, he made both *in his image.* What does that mean? It means that your life, in profound and mysterious ways, reflects the life of God. Art offers a glimpse of the artist. A poem is an echo of the poet's mind. You are the masterpiece of God. Like God, you are creative, intelligent, spiritual, relational, and beautiful. Imago Dei: in his image. No wonder God said, "It is good."

And yet, like the rest of creation, God made us with limits. Yes, we were formed in his image, but we don't have his divine essence. We're like God, but we're not God. I recently saw a new translation of Genesis inspired by Kanye West called *The Book of Yeezus*. In every place where the word *God* would have been is the word *Kanye*. Whoever made this may have taken Kanye's song "I Am a God" too literally, but I don't think even Kanye could create something from nothing!

And that's the remarkable thing about the creation story: a spiritual being created physicality, and then he placed us in it.

"Now the LORD God had planted a garden in the east, in Eden; and there he put the man" (Genesis 2:8).

The word *Eden* in Hebrew (עֵדֶן) means "delight." It was a place of unparalleled beauty, pulsating with the radiance of God. He spoke, and the earth twisted in life, plants stretched out their leaves, trees lifted their branches to the sky. He embellished the garden with flowers. He adorned the heavens with stars and filled the sea with fish. The seventeenth-century poet John Milton described Eden as a "delicious paradise."[2] Not quite heaven but the closest thing yet.

Still, as good as this garden was, it had very real limits. There were physical limits: boundaries and barriers that defined its location in the world. There were limits of time: the sun rose and set, days turned into weeks, months, years. There were moral limits: the garden was virtually sin-free, except for a talking snake (where did *he* come from?). There were also limits to human freedom: Adam and Eve could eat anything—except for the fruit of the Tree of Knowledge of Good and Evil. In a world of *yeses* there was only one *no*.

But—and here's the point—there still was a no. There were limits—boundaries, restrictions, and barriers. It was good, but it wasn't perfect.

》《

So what does all of this mean? And what on earth does it have to do with a book on doubt?

Everything.

Because we live in a world of limits, we doubt.

Because we don't have all the answers, questions naturally arise:

What is God like? How can I know him? What is life's purpose? Which way should I go?

An anonymous fourteenth-century mystic once said that we find ourselves "in a cloud of unknowing." That is why we doubt. We don't always see the sky.

However, what we have to be reminded of here is that all of this was part of God's design. He purposefully made it like this. He built limits into the system. It wasn't an accident. He knew we would have to live with so many unknowns. And yet he chose for the human story to look this way. Author Ronald Rolheiser wrote, "Every choice is a thousand renunciations. To choose one thing is to turn one's back on many others."[3] When God decided to create, he could have said yes to a thousand other possibilities. But he didn't. He chose this world. He chose you. He chose me. Limits and all. And still, he called it "good."

All of this means that doubts are normal.

They're a natural consequence of living in this world.

You doubt not because you're a terrible person or because you're less spiritual than everyone else. You doubt because you're human.

This is important, because so many Christians view doubt as if it were an unspeakable, repulsive sin. I once saw a television interview where a well-known pastor was asked whether he ever doubted. He looked horrified, as if he had just been asked if he enjoyed chain-smoking and late-night binging on marijuana brownies. "Of course not!" he retorted. In his view doubt represented a flaw of character or an in-your-face rebellion against God.

Why do people think this way?

One reason is related to our cultural obsession with certainty.

We want to know everything, all the time. We map the world with GPS because we want to see where everything is. We seek answers on Yelp because we want assurance the food is good. Every second we ask Google forty thousand questions globally.[4] Easy answers are just a few taps away. And, for the most part, we love it. We've tasted the tree of knowledge, and we keep coming back for more.

But this can be toxic for our faith. If all we care about is certainty, we lose the beauty of mystery. If all we value is explanation, we lose the joy of exploration. Deep faith is about progress, not perfection. But a glance at Christian subculture reveals what we prefer: our bookstores are stacked with resources that accentuate quick answers and easily memorized proofs. Our songs are replete with affirmations. Even our sermons are neatly structured models of industry: three didactic points, all beginning with the letter *p*. The benefit of this kind of Christianity is that all the work is already done for you. Just sign on the line and never worry about faith again. It's all highly structured and systematized; certainty has become the blueprint for our faith. No wonder Christians who draw outside the lines feel so unloved.

Another reason has to do with the way we've read (or misread) Genesis. Sadly, many have used the opening chapters of the Bible as a pretext to shame those who question their faith. We've literally demonized doubt. How so? Well, if you skip Genesis 1 and your starting point is Genesis 3, then doubt is a satanic lie, a catastrophic byproduct of the fall. I can't tell you how many sermons I've heard and books I've read that suggest doubt is somehow our fault: "Doubt came into the world the moment Adam and Eve ate the forbidden fruit." "Doubt is always a sin." "Doubt reveals that something is wrong with your character." The solution? Confess the sin of doubt and "just believe." Doubt ought to be repressed and denied. Push it back into the shadows. Anesthetize it with more church gatherings, songs, sermons, and statements of faith.

The downside to this, of course, is that suppressed doubt has a propensity to reemerge, often in a form far more volatile than before. And if that's the narrative we believe, should we be surprised when Christians who struggle with doubt feel they have no place in church? Should we be shocked when the questions they've concealed for years suddenly materialize and they announce on Snapchat that they're walking away from their faith?

The fall of humanity is a vital element of the Genesis story, but it must be interpreted in light of chapter 1. Starting there, not three pages in, reveals that doubt is part of the package. God didn't create Adam and Eve with all the answers to life's hardest questions. Instead, he allowed space for them to explore, question, and learn. He cultivated a garden in which mystery could coexist alongside faith. This means that when we doubt, God isn't disappointed with us; he understands. Doubt is a natural response to the limitations of our knowledge.

I'm not saying we should be content with our doubt or not make every effort to mature in our faith. Nor am I saying all forms of doubt are good. In fact, maybe as a reaction to incomplete and judgmental attitudes toward doubt, some run the opposite way and give up on their faith entirely. They look back on their faith and ridicule what they used to believe, and then look down on those who still have traditional understandings of faith, assuming they're standing in the way of progress.

Deconstruction can be healthy, and sometimes even crucial for genuine faith to emerge, but it can only take you so far. Any two-year-old can tear up a room. The real challenge is having convictions strong enough to live by.

Not all expressions of doubt are healthy. Not all doubt is worth holding onto.

But doubt itself is normal.

We need to stop vilifying those who live in the tension of conflicted faith. Doubt isn't a malevolent demon that we need to exorcise out of our brothers and sisters with sanctimonious words. It's part of their story. It's part of my story. Jude 22 says, "Be merciful to those who doubt."

>> <<

This, of course, brings us back to the question *why?* Why would God make the world this way? Why would he create us knowing we would experience doubt? Those are loaded questions. And perhaps Socrates had the best response: "I am ignorant of what I do not know." But let me offer a suggestion: What if God made the world like this to push us to deeper faith?

Frederick Buechner wrote, "Doubts are the ants in the pants of faith. They keep it awake and moving."[5] I love that. Doubts can amplify our thirst for truth. For reality. They're a doorway to intimacy. Doubts aren't just an obstacle; they're an opportunity. Uncertainty can lead us into the beautiful mystery we call God.

Jesus said the Spirit of God is like a wind that blows where it wishes (John 3:8). Wind can be gentle and healing, like a peaceful breeze on a summer's day. Wind can also be a Category-5 hurricane that bulldozes everything in its path. David once said that God is our rest (Psalm 62:5). True, but he can also be the source of our distress. He is the answer, but he is also the question. He welcomes us home, then blows the house down. He is unconventional, unpredictable, unrestrained, wild—and he has a particular disdain for boxes. In fact, the last time someone put him in one, he broke out three days later.

Because God is always on the move, then it follows that our faith will be too. The story is told of Augustine, the brilliant fourth-century theologian, who was once walking along the beach lost in thought. He was attempting to wrap his mind around a theological question. He then saw a boy scurrying back and forth, carrying a seashell of water, emptying it into a hole he had dug in the sand. Augustine asked what he was doing. The boy told him: he was transporting the entire sea into the hole. Augustine laughed. That's impossible! But then he realized that's what he had been trying to do with God.

Just when we think we've got God figured out, he vanishes. The more of him we let into our lives, the faster he soaks through the limits of our understanding. And that's why faith isn't about getting God to fit into our holes in the sand; it's about running to him. He calls us not to the shore, but the ocean. He invites us to move past our fear and into his heart, deeper and deeper, until we experience his presence around us and in us.

Faith isn't about containment, it's about possibility. Faith is skin-on-skin closeness, affinity, relationship. But to get there, sometimes our certainties need to be shattered. Our formulas disrupted. Our questions unanswered. And it's there, in the depths of relationship, that we encounter not a list of religious clichés, but a person. Friendship is born.

My wife Elyssa and I first met in the lobby of a church in the tiny town of Ruch, Oregon. Marriage has been an incredible ride. As we've done life together, I've learned a ton about who she is. I know her tastes, interests, hopes, anxieties, and (mostly!) can predict her moods. She used to be a cat person, but then we got a goldendoodle and she turned from the dark side. She likes flowers and nature and interior design. She's a morning person, loves to paint, and is extroverted until she spends time with people. She's kind, funny, and inexplicably loves sweet potatoes. She's an amazing woman, and I married way out of my league.

What I love about our relationship is that, although I know so much about her, there is still so much I'm learning. There are aspects to her story I'm just beginning to appreciate, glimpses of her personality that astonish me, ways she sees the world that I don't expect. In so many ways, she is still an enigma to me.

Now, because I haven't figured her out, should I be alarmed? Should I worry that the relationship is unhealthy or broken? Do we need counseling? That's one way of looking at it. Another perspective is that the ambiguity in our relationship is actually a sign of health, passion, and a friendship that is moving forward. Certainty can restrict love. But subtlety gives it room to flourish.

Consider beauty. Something is truly sublime when it takes you by surprise. You catch your breath and you can't take your eyes away; you didn't see it coming. Or think about humor. Wit is the art of verbalizing the unexpected. You laugh because it's not anticipated.

Unknowns are what make life so unspeakably rich, iridescent, and engaging.

If I literally knew everything about my wife—every thought, insight, emotion, move, and placement of every atom—not only would that be slightly creepy, but it would also hinder the progression of love. For example, why ask her questions if I already know the answer? What is there to learn? Why seek her if she's already been found? It's because I *don't* know everything that the relationship feels so alive. There are secrets waiting to be unearthed.

Questions aching to be asked. Dimensions of her I have yet to fully explore or understand. It's the pursuit of love that leads to the discovery of love.

Mystery is the lifeblood of intimacy.

The same thing is true in our relationship with God.

What if God intentionally created a world in which doubt exists because he knew it would open the door to lasting, authentic love? What if God designed it in such a way—seeing "through a glass, darkly" (1 Corinthians 13:12 KJV)—so we would ache to see him face-to-face? What if the meaning is in the longing? It's easy to love God when he seems so close; but true love is the pursuit of love. The desire for his presence pushes us to greater depths.

If God is infinite, then there are infinite dimensions about him to discover. Which means all it takes is a little obscurity, combined with curiosity, and the journey of faith begins.

Which brings us back to Genesis.

When God first spoke into the darkness, boundaries, limits, questions, and doubts came to be. That's the world we live in. But here's the interesting bit: God also made us curious. He built margins into the fabric of existence, but he also gave us an insatiable thirst to experience what lies beyond. He gave us a yearning for adventure, a passion to grow, a longing to explore. We were made to be pilgrims, not campers. A camper is content to stay in one location. A pilgrim, however, keeps moving, keeps breaking new ground, relentlessly chases unfamiliar terrain, and won't stop seeking new things.

I've always been intrigued by Genesis 2:19, which says God brought the animals "to the man to see what he would name them." What's surprising about this verse is that Adam was given complete freedom to identify, interact with, and study the natural world. God didn't give him a rigid set of instructions telling him how to label an iguana or giraffe. No, he gave Adam space to think, design, and create. Curiosity drove Adam's engagement with the complexity and miracle of life. And I can't help but wonder, was God curious too? The verse says he wanted to see what Adam would come up with!

The point is, curiosity is a gift from God. Curiosity, along with mystery, lies at the heart of creation. Curiosity pounds at the door of imagination. It fuels creativity, spiritual renewal, depth in relationships, scientific innovations, and the pursuit of truth. Curiosity gives birth to worship. Albert Einstein affirms,

> The most beautiful thing we can experience is the mysterious. It is the source of all true art and science. He to whom the emotion is a stranger, who can no longer pause to wonder and stand wrapped in awe, is as good as dead—his eyes are closed. This insight into the mystery of life . . . is at the center of true religiousness.[6]

That is what God invites us to step into. Celebrate mystery. Dance with curiosity. Resist the status quo. You're a pilgrim; explore. It is better to encounter God on the threshold of risk than to lose him in the comfort of mediocrity. Probe, wrestle, pursue, inquire. Ask the questions no one is willing to ask.

Perhaps you'll find out something new. Or maybe the answer will sound something like "big-fala hut, big-fala rat." But either way, you're still sitting around the fire. With friends. Laughing. Growing. Learning. Being surprised.

And that is what trust, and faith, is all about.

Chapter 2

Between Two Worlds

Doubt is a state of mind in suspension
between faith and unbelief.
—Os Guinness

I . . . am a heathen in my reason and a Christian
with my whole heart. I swim between two bodies
of water which will not unite so that together they
can hold me up, but while one continuously holds
me, the other is constantly letting me sink.
—Friedrich Heinrich Jacobi

THE AMERICAN NOVELIST AND art critic John Updike once said that a good story should take you "right up to the edge."[1] In other words, it entices you with mystery, which creates a synergy and expectation that keeps you coming back for more. Think Netflix binge meets three-day weekend: you lose track of time and possibly everything else because you're lost too. What I love about stories like that is the palpable sense that things could go either way. They defy simplistic, easily resolved narratives and ideas.

Instead, they invite you to step into the unknown, where the air is heavy with tension and everything hangs in the balance. You keep watching, desperate to know what happens, but at the same time you don't want it to end. We were made for stories like that.

One of my favorite stories is "The Country of the Blind" by H. G. Wells.[2] It describes the adventures of an Ecuadorian explorer named Nunez. One day, while attempting to summit the Parascotopetl Mountains, Nunez slipped and fell down the side of a steep and snowy embankment. Though stunned, he miraculously survived. After a night of rest, he awoke to the sound of singing birds and a sight that took his breath away. Nunez was in the middle of a sumptuous, mysterious valley cut off from the rest of the world by jagged, imposing cliff walls. He walked farther in and discovered a village whose inhabitants were all blind. Years before, they had been struck by an irreversible disease that slowly spread throughout the village. The sickness was passed on generation to generation, so that years later, not only had the villagers lost their sight, they had lost all memory of what it meant to see.

Nunez felt sorry for them and tried to explain what their home was like. He told them that they lived in a valley that was astoundingly beautiful, opulent in color and diversity. He described the sky, clouds, and stars. He told them about the delicate intricacy of flowers, the wonder of snow-capped mountains, the staggering elegance of a sunrise. However, the more he spoke, the more the villagers were mystified by his story. They thought he was lying. Some thought he was deluded. A few mocked him. Philosophers interrogated him with questions. The village doctors even offered to take out his eyes to "cure" him of his madness. Nunez finally realized that many in the village simply didn't want to believe the truth. Because of their blindness, they assumed that their perspective was all that existed.

It wasn't long before Nunez began to question himself. As the villagers challenged him, his own mind raced with doubts. He struggled to make sense of what was real. What if what they were saying was right? What if all that he was seeing was a hallucination? Could it be that he had been living a lie? It's like that scene from *The Matrix* when Neo wakes up in a cocoon. His assurance of what the world looked like was disrupted; nothing made sense anymore.

Adding to the drama of the story, a few months later, Nunez fell in love with a gorgeous woman. He eagerly explained to her what it was like to see, insisting that he wasn't insane. She listened sympathetically, in the same way you might listen to a child describe her imaginary talking bear, but she didn't believe. She pressed him: lose your sight, let the doctors cure you of your sickness, and become blind like me. Let go of your delusions!

Nunez had to decide. Would he forgo his sight and gain the trust and love of this woman? Or would he keep his sight and run away?

» «

So what happened to Nunez? We'll get to that soon. But first, let's take a moment and consider how this story, in not only *how* it is told but *what* it describes, relates to doubt.

H. G. Wells brilliantly juxtaposes Nunez's deepest sense of what he thought was true with his deepest longing for love. Nunez was torn. The valley had caused him to question everything at a profound level. Who was right? Which path would he choose? What version of reality would he embrace? As the reader, it's impossible to predict the outcome. You're standing at the edge. You're swept up into the moment. The slightest push in either direction, and the story changes. Dramatically.

That is what doubt looks like.

Doubt is the interruption of your story when, like Nunez, everything you thought about God and faith is brought into question. Doubt is when you're torn by incompatible desires between what you feel and what you think. It's when the old narratives, the old ways of seeing reality no longer seem to work. You once were blind, but now you see—*or do you?* Doubt is the knife-edge, the limbo; you're caught between two worlds, and things could go either way.

The *Oxford Dictionary* defines doubt in similar terms. Doubt, it says, means "a feeling of uncertainty," or to "question the truth or fact of something."[3] It originates from the Latin word *dubitare*, which comes from an Aryan word meaning "two." So when you doubt, you are literally "in two minds." You vacillate between two opposing points of view. Os Guinness, in his book *God in the Dark*, writes, "This two-ness or double-ness is the heart of doubt and the deepest dilemma it presents. The heart of doubt is a divided heart."[4] He points out that when you study anthropology, you find that people have understood doubt this way. For example, the Greeks defined doubt as a tearing of the mind. The Chinese envisioned doubt as a man with a foot in two separate boats (that's not going to end well!). The Peruvians defined doubt as "having two thoughts," and in Guatemala, it's a person whose "heart is made two."[5] Likewise, the New Testament uses words for doubt that depict someone who is confused or conflicted between two paths. For example, James 1:6 says that the doubter is divided, "blown and tossed by the wind."

What's vital to note here is that when the Bible uses the word *doubt* it's different from the word *unbelief* (Matthew 14:31 and

Hebrews 3:19). This is important because some Christians assume that doubt and unbelief are synonymous. They're not. Doubt can lead to unbelief, just as doubt can lead to faith. But the two are not the same.

Doubt says, "I am unsure of what is right." Unbelief says, "I don't *care* about what is right."

Doubt is searching for the light. Unbelief is choosing to gouge out your eyes.

Doubt is pursuing truth, wherever it may lead. Unbelief is content with a lie.

Doubt exists somewhere between belief and unbelief. Doubt is the moment of tension, which in and of itself isn't good or bad. It's somewhere in between.

We all know what that feels like. As we saw in chapter 1, doubt is a reality because of the limits of our understanding. We live in the country of the blind. What's unique about our post-Christian age, however, is that the amount of voices telling us to lose our sight has increased. Dramatically.

We are endlessly pressured to reject belief. Or, at least, belief that actually shapes our life. Cynical thoughts, words, podcasts, movies, ideas, people, and experiences that feed our doubt inundate us. Bestselling books argue that faith in God is a delusion. A documentary exposes hypocrisy in the church. A professor says that stories in the Bible are nothing more than myth. A TV show ridicules people of faith. Social media often portrays Christians as uneducated, angry, and bigoted. Pluralism fosters the narrative that truth is relative.

The list goes on. Skepticism pulls on us, swirls around us, drags us under, pressures us into mainstream conformity.

Meanwhile, followers of Jesus are swimming upstream.

The author James K. A. Smith argues that believing doesn't come easy anymore: "We don't believe instead of doubting; we believe while doubting. We're all Thomas now."[6] The stats agree. A Pew survey revealed that the number of young Americans who experience doubts about God increased 15 percent in five years.[7] The Barna Group, which studies social movements and trends, records that two-thirds of people who self-identify as Christian have struggled with doubt, millennials experience doubt twice as much as any other generational group,[8] and Gen Z (the generation following the millennials) is considered the least Christian generation in our nation's history.[9]

Like waves, we're assailed by doubts about God and faith. None of us are immune. We're uneasy, torn in two, gasping for air. We may still believe, but we wonder what our faith will look like when this is over.

In the next chapter, we'll talk about how disturbing and unsettling this can be. But for now, it's important to reemphasize that God does not shame us for having doubts. He does not blame us for our uncertainty. It's normal and natural. In many ways, it's inevitable. If the best stories are imbued with mystery, then God is an exceptional storyteller. Because there is so much that we don't yet know.

We also need to acknowledge that while our cultural moment ferments the deconstruction of faith, we can capitalize on this moment in pursuit of deep faith. The existentialist philosopher Jean-Paul Sartre once said, "Man is condemned to be free."[10] That is, life was so much simpler when everyone interpreted reality the same way as you, when everyone was blind like you, or when there was only one way to think. But the moment a blind philosopher shows up, you're haunted by the question, *What if I'm wrong?*

Some interpret that question as an attack on faith. But what if this moment is faith's greatest opportunity? Maybe we need to be challenged so our opinions and beliefs can be examined and renewed. Maybe the pressures we feel as followers of Jesus are cultivating grace for those who struggle to believe, and creating space for a more vibrant, culturally-engaged faith to grow. Historically, God's people have found their voice in exile. It's where much of the Bible was written. It's where revolutions began. Identity is born in the agony of exclusion. And once identity is discovered, the uniqueness, otherness, and beauty of its counter-narrative draws an unbelieving world back to itself.

If that's true, it means we don't have to panic when the world throws doubt in our face. There's nothing to fear. And there's nothing to fear when we encounter doubt of any kind, or from any source. Whether it's the pressures of culture, the tragic circumstances of life, the fluctuations of emotion, the growing pains of spiritual formation, or some hidden inner angst, when doubt interrupts your journey, you need to appreciate its potential to move you forward in ways you never have before.

Doubt isn't the end of the story; it's the suspense within it. Doubt is the unexpected mystery; an unresolved, lingering question. Doubt is when you're fixed on the edge of your seat, uneaten popcorn sitting in your open mouth, clawing your neighbor's arm, unable to take your eyes off the screen although you wish you could.

Doubt presses you to reevaluate the story of your life. What are your values? What do you really believe? What direction do you want to go? Like water between two banks, doubt creates space for diverging outcomes.[11] You can swim toward God or away. You can reach toward belief or unbelief. The choice is yours. Doubt is essentially neutral; it's what you do with it that counts.

» «

For me, two fascinating individuals who illustrate the power and potential of doubt are Mother Teresa and Friedrich Nietzsche. I know. It's almost an oxymoron seeing their two names together. Like *bittersweet*. Act natural. Or Dodge Ram. They couldn't have been more dramatically different. But, surprisingly, they both began their journey in a spiritually similar place, until doubt disrupted their life's trajectory. Let me share with you a bit of their story.

MOTHER TERESA

Years ago, I visited India. As I exited the plane, my senses exploded. The sights, sounds, colors, heat, and beauty bombarded me. It was electric. I saw cows walking down busy streets, people washing their clothes in the Ganges River, merchants attempting to sell obvious imitations of designer brands. (I saw a pair of shoes with NIEK written on the side!) There were monkeys everywhere. One, and this is so stereotypical, actually stole a banana I was eating. Anything could happen in India. And I *loved* it.

The second week I was there, I took a train from Delhi to Calcutta to spend time at Mother Teresa's mission: the Kalighat Home for the Dying. It's essentially a hospice, a place of refuge for those who are in the final days of their lives. And it's open to anyone. People came in off the streets with a range of diseases and debilitations. I'll never forget the compassion and tangible displays of kindness shown by the nuns who worked there. Day after day, they selflessly served the sick and dying, caring for their needs, feeding them, bathing them, embracing them with hope, tears, and prayer. One man had been horribly injured, his arm sliced open by a machete. The open wound was infected and covered with maggots. Fighting nausea, I started to turn away but stopped when I caught the eyes of the nun who was caring for him. She had so much warmth and empathy. She prayed for him. She sang to him. She smiled as she tenderly washed out his wound. Where others had turned away from the sick and dying, these nuns embraced them with unrelenting love. It was beautiful to see.

Mother Teresa's mission was clear: "The poor must be loved, because they have been created by the loving hand of God to love and be loved."[12] Her faith in God was simple, unpretentious, and the source of inspiration for countless people throughout the world.

What many people don't realize, however, is that while Mother Teresa possessed deep faith, she also struggled with deep doubt. At times, overwhelmingly so. Ten years after her death, a book of her personal letters was published, called *Come Be My Light: The Private Writings of the Saint of Calcutta*. In one of these letters, she expressed her devastating journey into doubt:

> Where is my faith? Even deep down, right in, there is nothing but emptiness and darkness. My God, how painful is this unknown pain. It pains without ceasing . . . I dare not utter the words and thoughts that crowd my heart and make me suffer untold agony. So many unanswered questions live within me.[13]

These questions tore into her heart. For decades, Mother Teresa wrestled with intense seasons of loneliness. She wondered why God seemed so consistently absent from her life and if her suffering meant anything at all. She cried out to him. She swam in the waters of doubt.

And yet, rather than moving away from God, she allowed her doubts to lead her toward God. She chose to believe in the God she couldn't understand. She leaned into the mystery of faith, eyes open in search of truth. Her faith gave her sight, bringing into focus the beauty in others, which then mobilized her to serve the poor and wounded. She once said, "Faith in action is love. And love in action is service."[14]

Her life reminds me of a story in *Works of Love* by Søren Kierkegaard. He compares the perspective of two artists who were seeking inspiration. One traveled extensively and saw innumerable people but found nobody worth painting. In his view, they weren't perfect enough. The other artist, however, remained in his hometown and had no problem finding people to paint. Why? Because he recognized beauty in everyone.[15] Such was the perspective of Mother Teresa. Her faith animated her sight. She explained,

> I see Jesus in every human being. I say to myself, this is hungry Jesus, I must feed him. This is sick Jesus. This one has leprosy or gangrene; I must wash him and tend to him. I serve because I love Jesus.[16]

Mother Teresa decided that the best way to live was to see Jesus in others and to celebrate his presence in the world. Though part of her screamed for greater clarity, she still affirmed God's reality and refused to let her doubts win.

FRIEDRICH NIETZSCHE

If Mother Teresa was one of the most influential Christians of her time, then the philosopher Friedrich Nietzsche was one of the most influential atheists. His works are simultaneously tragic, sarcastic, adversarial, affirming, inspiring, evocative, and confusing. I once heard someone say that reading Nietzsche is the intellectual equivalent of speaking in tongues. The only difference is that with Nietzsche, there is no interpretation!

What fascinates me about Nietzsche is his tumultuous spiritual journey and the way he was haunted by faith and doubt.

Nietzsche was born on October 15, 1844. He grew up in a small German town and was the oldest of three children. His father, Carl Ludwig, was a pastor who died from a tortuous brain disease when Nietzsche was just five years old. For years, Nietzsche wrestled with his father's suffering. How could a good God allow such a thing to happen? This was the dawn of a journey into doubt that would define Nietzsche for the rest of his life.

At the age of twenty, he enrolled at the University of Bonn with the hopes of becoming a pastor like his father. After one semester, however, he abruptly dropped out, announcing that he had lost his faith. His early writings reveal that he embraced biblical criticism, a new method of study that questioned the Bible's historical legitimacy. If his father's suffering caused him to reject God emotionally, biblical criticism motivated him to reject God intellectually.

His mother was heartbroken by the news.

In 1882 he wrote "The Parable of the Madman" and famously stated, "God is dead."

I once saw street art where someone had spray-painted "God is dead," signed "Nietzsche." Someone later came and crossed it out, writing, "Nietzsche is dead," signed "God." Ironic, especially considering what Nietzsche meant by his parable. He wrote it because he firmly believed that the demise of theism was near. It was time for society to throw off the shackles of belief and embrace the freedom of a life without God. Nietzsche wasn't saying that life without him would be easy. In fact, he argued, rejecting God would have disturbing consequences socially, politically, personally, and especially morally. In his book *Twilight of the Idols*, he wrote,

> When one gives up the Christian faith, one pulls the right to Christian morality out from under one's feet. This morality is by no means self-evident . . . Christianity is a system, a whole view of things thought out together. By breaking one main concept out of it, the faith in God, one breaks the whole.[17]

In other words, belief in God matters. Ideas have consequences. It's one thing to casually announce on social media that you don't believe in God. You may even get a ton of likes and affirmations for being authentic. But when you actually try and live it out, you'll find that it has all kinds of real-world implications.

Nietzsche said if you gaze long into an abyss, the abyss will also gaze into you.[18] What you choose to believe influences the trajectory of your life. Nietzsche chose unbelief, and he tried to bring as many people with him as possible.

A few years later, while visiting a friend in Turin, Nietzsche had a mental breakdown. Although most historians attribute this event to syphilis, some scholars such as A. J. Hoover and the philosopher Georges Bataille argued his breakdown was connected to his ideology. Could it be that his atheism, and his insistence that there was no ultimate meaning in life, created a psychological disruption? A few years earlier, he had written, "O ye heavenly powers, grant me madness! . . . I am devoured by doubt."[19]

In Turin, these words may have become a self-fulfilling prophecy.

Regardless of what caused his mental collapse, it's clear Nietzsche wrestled profusely with the reality of God. Some hail Nietzsche as the iconic atheist. A man standing firm in the face of belief, refusing to back down. But there's another way of looking at it. It's been said that the opposite of love isn't hate, it is indifference. True atheists not only disbelieve in God; they are genuinely disinterested in the idea of him. They're aloof and disengaged. But Nietzsche was anything but nonchalant when it came to God. He denounced what he thought couldn't exist. He hated what he didn't believe was real. He sought to distance himself from God, but something inside him wouldn't let it go.

Shakespeare may have said it best when he wrote: "The lady doth protest too much, methinks."[20]

>> <<

You couldn't find two more strikingly different stories than those of Mother Teresa and Friedrich Nietzsche.

One was a nun, the other a philosopher.

One took a vow of chastity; the other contracted syphilis in a brothel.

One saw God in the chaos and beauty of life; the other said, "God is dead."

One lived in poverty, serving the poor; the other relished a life of affluence.

One died in peace, the other in madness.

Two totally different lives. And yet, what they had in common was that they both experienced a crisis of faith. They both encountered difficult and frightening questions about God. They both asked: *Where is God? Why is there suffering? How do I know his Word is true?* Doubt, like angry waves, besieged them.

And yet, one moved toward belief. The other toward unbelief.

It's worth saying again: doubt is the neutral space between belief and unbelief. Doubt pushes us, urges us, prompts us, pressures us; we swim in its waters. But, ultimately, we decide which way we want to go. Some, like Nietzsche, use their doubts to justify rejection of God. Others, like Mother Teresa, harness their doubts toward a more beautiful and flourishing faith. But either way you're in the driver's seat.

The Welsh preacher Martyn Lloyd-Jones said, "Doubts are not incompatible with faith. . . . Some people seem to think that once you become a Christian you should never be assailed by doubts. But that is not so . . . Doubts will attack us, but that does not mean that we are to allow them to master us."[21]

Just because you have questions doesn't mean you're losing your faith.

Just because there are things you don't understand about God doesn't mean that he doesn't exist.

Just because you hurt doesn't mean that God doesn't care.

God is with you in the doubt. He understands. He's been there.

In the Garden of Gethsemane, Jesus cried out to his Father, "If it is possible, let this cup pass from me!" His body was aching with doubt. He sweat drops of blood. His fingers dug into the dirt. He was confused, worried, unsure.

But then he prayed, "Not my will be done, but yours." He chose to believe. And because of that, we have redemption.

In another garden, Adam and Eve were enchanted by two trees, and one was forbidden. Doubt filled their hearts. They could taste the fruit in their mouths.

They turned away from their Creator and ate. And because of that, we have sin, sadness, suffering, war, racism, injustice. Everything that's wrong with the world.

Two gardens. Two choices. Two stories of doubt.

And not a day goes by when we're not in the garden too.

Like Adam and Eve, we live between two trees, torn between competing desires. Belief on one side, unbelief on the other. The air is heavy with tension. Everything hangs in the balance.

Part of us wonders why God made it that way. Why does God allow us to doubt at all? We've explored the idea of intimacy in chapter 1, and I'm sure there are other reasons too.

Maybe it's because doubt humbles us and shows us how far we have to go.

Maybe it's because our limitation is God's invitation. He pulls us into deeper truth.

Or maybe it's just because God loves a good story. And, as you know, a good story is never boring and predictable, but full of suspense, unknowing, and even fear.

It's Jesus weeping in Gethsemane. It's Mother Teresa wrestling with her doubts. It's Nunez choosing between love and sight.

Which brings us back to the Country of the Blind. The last time we saw Nunez, he was confronted by the most excruciating decision of his life. Would he become blind and marry the village woman, or would he keep his eyes and run away?

What's fascinating is that H. G. Wells wrote several different endings to his book! One says that Nunez returned for the woman; another says that he immediately left the village. There's even a version where he and the woman ran away together, bought a tiny house in Portland, and started a vegan food truck that sold imitation llama burgers. (Just kidding, I made that last bit up.)

When I first saw this, I couldn't believe it! I wanted to know the real ending. After all, I like closure. I want all the tangled threads tied together in a neat and tidy way. But as I began to think about it, I realized the uncertainty is what makes the story so compelling.

It's not perfectly resolved, because neither is life. It's chaotic and confusing and hopeful and bursting with possibilities because, for whatever reason, that's how the storyteller designed it to be.

Nunez was caught between two worlds. And we are too. Which way will you choose? Will you move toward God or away? Will you keep your eyes or become blind?

You get to decide how the story ends.

Chapter 3

When the Sun Goes Dark

The sea of faith
Was once, too, at the full, and round earth's shore
Lay like the folds of a bright girdle furl'd.
But now I only hear
Its melancholy, long, withdrawing roar,
Retreating, to the breath
Of the night-wind, down the vast edges drear
And naked shingles of the world.
—MATTHEW ARNOLD, "DOVER BEACH"

My hosanna is born of a furnace of doubt.
—FYODOR DOSTOEVSKY

IT WAS THE KIND of event that only happens once every fifty years. I grabbed my camera, coffee, a couple of protein bars, and jumped into my friend's car. We drove south for about forty-five minutes, then pulled over next to a quiet field, set up our cameras, and waited.

I've seen solar eclipses before, but this one was different. It was a full eclipse. We were in the path of totality, and it was about to happen right here, in my home state of Oregon. I was so excited. There are a lot of unrealistic things on my bucket list, like seeing emperor penguins in Antarctica, exploring Italy with a Leica camera, and watching the finals at Wimbledon. But at least the eclipse had a reasonable chance of happening.

We kept checking our watches, sipping our coffee, and waiting for the show to begin.

Finally, it was time.

The moon slowly began to gnaw away at the sun, giving it a cute Pac-Man motif. I put on my cheap cardboard eclipse sunglasses and watched as the drama unfolded. What immediately caught me by surprise was how little the earth was affected at first. The sun was still bright. It felt warm. Nothing about the day seemed out of place or different. Even when the eclipse was at 80 percent, nothing changed.

I'm not sure what I expected to happen. I had read intriguing stories of eclipses in history. In ancient China, people believed that dragons were eating the sun and would angrily shout and bang pots and drums to scare the dragons away. In Assyria, a five-minute eclipse led to an insurrection in the city of Ashur, and in 557 BC, the historian Xenophon recorded how an eclipse terrified the inhabitants of the city Larissa, who abandoned it to the invading Persians.

In Oregon, there were no dragons, invading Persians, or pots (although a few people sitting nearby might have been smoking some!). It was almost anticlimactic. But what happened next I can only describe as one of the most surreal experiences of my life. Moments before the total eclipse, the world turned to dusk. The temperature rapidly dropped. Birds hurriedly flew back to their nests. The landscape looked muted and Mars-like. It was as if the *sun* was wearing sunglasses. The wind started to blow, rustling the leaves around us.

And then, suddenly, all went dark. Full totality. Against my better judgment and everything I'd read about eclipses, I took off my glasses and looked up. I couldn't help it. There, hanging in the sky like a circular phantom meets Death Star, was a massive orb, the moon. It looked close and intimidating, yet emphatically beautiful. Blazing out from its sides, in every direction, streams of sunlight poured spectacularly into space. It felt like the moon was being overcome, swallowed up in luminescence, and was trying everything in its power to hold itself together.

Unexpectedly, I struggled to hold myself together too. (If you've ever seen a total eclipse, you'll know what I'm talking about.) It was as if my emotions were suddenly raw, muddled, and swept up by the gravity of the sun. My heart raced as I felt my sense of reality shift, my perceptions displaced. It was hypnotic, mesmerizing, and disorienting. I attempted to capture some pictures on my Nikon but kept losing myself in the moment. There were so many sensations: awe, wonder, fear, amazement, worry—so much to take in. And then, moments after it began, it was all over.

Clinical psychologist Kate Russo is famous for studying the emotional impact of eclipse-watchers. After years of interviewing and collecting stories from people, she invented the acronym SPACED to describe the stages of emotion a person goes through: a Sense of wrongness, Primal fear, Awe, Connection, Euphoria, and the Desire to repeat the event.[1] SPACED is definitely a good way of describing what I felt that day forty-five minutes south of Portland. And if you saw me afterward, it's probably a good acronym for what I looked like too.

I am so thankful to have experienced it.

I'm so glad they don't happen every day.

And I'm so wanting to fly to South America when it happens again.

» «

In the last chapter, we looked at how doubt is essentially neutral. It's when your assumptions about what the world looks like are brought into question. That moment in and of itself isn't good or bad. It can move you toward deeper belief or unbelief.

But there is one important point to make here. Yes, doubt is neutral in principle. But it's anything but neutral in the way it *feels*.

When you experience doubt, it's as if the sun has gone dark.

It's disruptive, confusing, and sometimes agonizing.

Doubt is the eclipse of certainty. It's when the old answers or ways of doing things no longer sustain you. It's a feeling of spiritual, mental, and even physical nausea. Doubt is vertigo.

Of course, all of this is normal and natural. But this doesn't lessen the pain. Because the fact is, doubt can be an undoing of everything that you trust and hold dear. It hurts.

A place in Scripture that puts this on display is the book of Psalms. In fact, some of the most raw and passionate expressions of doubt ever written are found there. This may be a surprise to some, since much of Western Christian subculture has flattened the Psalms to just words of encouragement we read when we're going through a hard time. If we need a quick fix as we head out the door, we swiftly ingest a psalm; it's an easy pick-me-up, a double shot of vanilla for our spiritual latte.

Now, it's true there's plenty of refreshment in the Psalms. The verses spill over with encouragement and hope. But what we often overlook is that the Psalms engage our struggles too. They weren't written just to anesthetize our wounds but to invite us redemptively into them. The Psalms are brooding, thoughtful, and unafraid to grapple with experiences of spiritual and emotional darkness. Many are exceedingly heavy and true to life, expressing in-the-moment disappointment and frustration with God. The language of doubt pervades them. In the book *Spirituality of the Psalms,* the brilliant Old Testament scholar Walter Brueggemann makes the argument that the 150 poems in Psalms essentially fall into three different categories:[2]

PSALMS OF ORIENTATION. These are songs that were written in seasons of celebration and worship. The author expressed awe in a loving God who not only delights in his creation, but who relentlessly invades every space in it with his beauty and presence. He was grateful that the same Creator loved and delighted in him too. God's favor and peace imbue these psalms, and the author relished in them. Wonder, amazement, joy, and gratitude pour off the pages (see Psalms 8, 24, and 33).

PSALMS OF DISORIENTATION. These songs came out of a place of unexpected disruption, when anger, despair, suffering, and tragedy eclipsed the author's faith in God (see Psalms 13, 22, 32, and 51). They're gritty, uncensored, and unapologetically honest. A piercing example of this is Psalm 130, which opens with a scream: "Out of the depths I cry to you." In Latin, the phrase "out of the depths" is *de profundis,* which means hurt, grief, confusion, fear, anger, and doubt. If you've spent much time in literature, *de profundis* might ring a bell. It was the title of a famous letter written by the poet Oscar Wilde when he was in prison. It's also been used as the name for ballets, musicals, compositions, poems, songs, movies, apps, perfumes, and board games. There's even a Polish death metal album with that name. Interesting how a simple Latin phrase taken from a three-thousand-year-old psalm can resonate with us so well.

PSALMS OF NEW ORIENTATION. These songs, like a seedling rises through broken soil, were written to express faith reborn. The doubt lingered on, but the author harnessed its energy to move toward belief rather than unbelief. There is a fresh sense of clarity, as if the fog had finally lifted and glimpses of God were visible once more. When you read these psalms (see Psalms 23, 27, 56, and 91), you'll notice a courageous resolve and a searing awareness of purpose in the author's words. He chose to trust in God despite the pain he experienced: "When I am afraid, I put my trust in you" (Psalm 56:3).

Dividing the book of Psalms this way is not only a brilliant approach to understanding an ancient book, but it's also an effective blueprint that describes our journey of faith. If you've been walking with Jesus for long, you know that life, like the Psalms, involves three spiritual movements: orientation, disorientation, and new orientation. Orientation is when you feel at home. The theological framework you were handed from your parents or church simply works. You feel secure in your relationship with God, confident in the integrity of your faith. Disorientation changes all that. It's when doubt, like an unwelcome, volatile arsonist, bursts through the door and sets fire to your faith. You watch bewildered as your rooted beliefs, theology, and ideas about God burn to the ground. New orientation, however, is when you stand in the ashes of what used to be, and then you start to rebuild. The taste of ash lingers in your mouth and the air is thick with smoke, yet you inexplicably see Jesus in ways you never did before. Home is different now, and part of you is too, but surprisingly, you're thankful for what you just experienced.

The book of Psalms is God's way of saying, "I get it. I understand. And I'm with you through it all." The Psalms speak to us and they speak for us. They give our doubts a voice.

Psalm 73 is another stunning example of what this looks like. This poem was written by a worship leader named Asaph, and it begins with the faith-filled affirmation, "Truly God is good" (NKJV). To this day, I can't read that line without thinking of churches I've been to where someone cheerfully shouts from the stage, "God is good!" and the congregation shouts back, "All the time, God is good!" Now, that may be true theologically, but it can come off sounding like you're being handed a winner's script. Or worse, a churchy version of *The Lego Movie*: "Everything is awesome!" But here's the problem: everything isn't always awesome. Life can be tragic and hard. All around us people suffer. The world is fragmented and lonely. The Lego gospel isn't enough.

And that is why Psalm 73 is so provocative. Asaph didn't stop with simple assertions of God's goodness. In the verses that follow he listed a range of brutal objections to God's character and power: the wicked flourish and there is no justice (vv. 3–12), all my attempts at doing good are in vain (v. 13), and life is filled with suffering (v. 14). Notice that the affirmation of God's goodness lies alongside the reality of doubt; both are given room to breathe in the same song. Yes, God is good. But often we don't feel his goodness. According to H. G. Enelow, a rabbi and Jewish scholar,

There are times when the very foundations of the Psalmist's faith are shaken by actual experience—by what happens to him, or in the world at large—and that is what opens the door to doubt; not the doubt of the proud and scornful, not arrogant doubt, but pensive doubt, the doubt of the wounded and baffled, though faithful, soul.[3]

Doubt is emotional and spiritual disorientation. It is, according to Asaph, the moment when our feet begin to slip.

Recently, I took our goldendoodle, Bella, for a four-mile hike to Smith Rock. It's a popular place to visit in Oregon, and every year thousands of people explore, take photos, and adventurously gear up and climb many of its steep cliff walls. A friend of mine who is passionate about rock climbing once told me that while he loves the excitement of the climb, a single slip can change everything. In a moment, you can go from a euphoric high and exhilaration to overwhelming detachment and terror. As you slip, you clasp, clutch, claw, trying desperately to find something to hold on to. Vertigo sets in, and the world spins.

Doubt is like that. It's the moment in your life when what you thought was holding you up disintegrates, and you find yourself grasping thin air. It's when faith fails. You scramble for something solid and certain, but the earth gives way.

That's what Asaph was going through. He truly believed that God was good, but everything in his life was shouting the opposite. As he reached for certainty, he fell into the unremitting tension between what he thought he knew about God and the reality of his fractured life. It was tearing him apart: "My heart was grieved and my spirit embittered" (v. 21).

Why was this season of doubt so painful for Asaph? And why, when we doubt, is it so excruciating for us? One reason is that doubting can feel like a broken friendship. Have you ever been in a relationship with someone and heard or seen something in them that caught you off guard? Perhaps you saw them act way out of character. Or maybe you became aware of disturbing details in their past. Usually when that happens, you'll try to justify your presuppositions about them with what you've just learned. That can be incredibly disorienting and painful. And once you open that door, all sorts of other doubts about them come rushing in. Doubts create doubts. You wonder if the relationship will ever be the same again.

Your relationship with God defines who you are at the deepest level. As you walk with him and love him, you open your heart, pouring out your longings and desires. He listens. You walk more. And then you realize *he* is your longing and desire. He is your shepherd, and you want nothing else, just more of him. That is why throughout history, poets, writers, musicians, and artists have been so inspired to write, create, and sing of this God. Knowing him is the most beautiful love imaginable.

And that is what makes doubt so devastating. It feels like a loss of relationship or a fracturing of trust. You thought God was good. You thought your faith was true. But then doubt came and knocked you off your feet. Now everything is up in the air.

Your heart weeps.

In 1960 Joy Davidman, the wife of C. S. Lewis, passed away from a tragic battle with cancer. Although they had only been married for four years, Lewis described those years as the most beautiful of his life.[4] However, the depth of his affection for Joy while she lived meant a depth of sorrow unlike any he had ever experienced when she died. A year later, he published the book *A Grief Observed*. This short book is powerful, raw, elegant, and heartbreaking. In it Lewis pours out all his emotion in real time. There are no simple answers in the book, only ferocious questions.

He wondered where God was when he needed him most. He felt abandoned by his silence. His faith was wounded, and his doubt on full display.

But what created the most doubt within him were disconcerting questions about God's character. He wondered if God was not who he envisioned him to be. Lewis had believed in the God of Asaph: God is good! But maybe he was deceived. Was God indifferent? Was he malevolent? This thought terrified Lewis, but the suffering he experienced was so devastating that it genuinely felt like a callous betrayal. God was once an intimate friend, but now he seemed aloof and disinterested. Lewis was shattered. Like Asaph, his feet slipped as he struggled to cling to his faith. The world spun.

When Nietzsche wrote about the loss of faith, he, too, described it in terms of disorientation: "Are we not perpetually falling? Backward, sideward, forward, in all directions. . . . Are we not straying as through an infinite nothing?"[5] Doubt can make you feel like a spiritual orphan, displaced and sick for home.

And this isn't just felt at a spiritual level; doubt can have a notable effect upon our physical bodies too. Neurological studies have demonstrated that when we encounter perspectives that conflict with our beliefs, our bodies react. For example, when the amygdala, which controls our fight-or-flight reflex, is activated, blood pressure rises and our stress increases.[6] And this is just the beginning. Another academic paper entitled "Religious Doubts and Sleep Quality" explores the strain of doubt and its influence on the human body. It maintains that religious doubt can feed insomnia and depression and contribute to overall poor physical health.[7]

This shouldn't come as a huge surprise. When God created us, he made us as holistic, integrated beings. But if we bifurcate our beliefs from the rest of our lives, it impacts us in all sorts of ways: neurologically, physically, emotionally, spiritually. We're interconnected. So whenever cherished beliefs shatter, a part of us shatters too. Even the slightest eclipse of doubt casts a shadow throughout our lives.

>> <<

Like many of you, I know what this feels like. My experience with doubt began early in life. I was born in Oxford, England, and at the age of eight my family moved to Southern California, making me the awkward, reserved, British third-grader trying to fit into a world of surfers and valley-girl accents. I felt like a lone porpoise in a school of hyperactive dolphins.

Even though my parents weren't yet believers and the subject of religion rarely came up, I remember even then wrestling with the idea of God. I'll never forget one night when I was ten, lying awake in bed. It was a clear, beautiful evening, and I was gazing out my window at the stars. I whispered a prayer, asking God a simple question: "Do you really love me?" I had heard that he might, but I wanted to make sure. I followed up my prayer with a request: "If you do love me, would you mind letting me know by sending a shooting star?" (I had never seen one before.) It's a cheesy story I know, and I feel awkward even sharing it, but my prayer came from a place of innocent desire: I had to find out what God was like. Within seconds, I saw two shooting stars. I was stunned. I even cried for a bit. That moment meant so much to me.

Looking back on my story, I think I know why. In middle school, there was a ton of brokenness in my family. My parents were separated, my dad was struggling with alcohol and living in

San Diego, and my amazing mom was doing her best to raise my sister, Rebecca, and me. It was such a disorienting time.

Then my mom met Jesus. She started taking us to church. We heard messages from the Bible and learned about the gospel, and for the first time we began to have hope that God could restore our hurting family. I later attended my first Christian summer camp. On the last night, a youth pastor stood on a little platform in the woods and shared from his heart. More than a hundred middle schoolers sat on rustic benches, absorbing his words. He talked about grace, forgiveness, and the cross. Something in my heart gave, and when he invited us to respond, I raised my hand and surrendered my life to Jesus. My sister did the same soon after. Three of us had become Christians, and there was only one left. My dad was outnumbered! Every night, my sister, mom, and I would kneel on the ground to pray for him. We begged for healing, intervention, and miracles. We believed God could bring him home. And he did. Months later, my dad met Jesus, too, and his life (and my parents' marriage) began to be put back together.

I don't want to pretend that everything was perfect from then on. It wasn't. But God's power to redeem is greater than sin's power to destroy. Grace always wins. I was awestruck by what God had done. I tried to learn everything about him that I could. I drank up the Bible's stories and words. Every possible chance, I was in church, listening, serving, participating. I was a youth group fanboy. I read books. I recorded radio sermons so that I could listen to them when I returned from school. I looked in awe upon those who were "in the ministry"; they seemed so close to God. In the midst of a stormy childhood, my faith was an anchor, a solace, a stable refuge. God was so real and near.

And yet, there were times of very real doubt too.

As I spent more time in the Bible, I loved it, but I was also confused. So many *begats*. So many sacrifices. Blood oozed from its pages. At first, I loved the drama and thrill of the war stories like those found in Joshua. But as I got older, I realized these were accounts of people suffering in unspeakably violent ways. Why would God allow that?

Other things confused me too: prayer, spiritual warfare, Christians who appeared so angry when they believed in a God of love, lack of unity in the church, other religions, the silence of God, forgiveness, and so on.

But mostly, I struggled to understand why a good God would allow so much pain in the world. And I'm not just talking about the obvious things like cancer and war but the wounds that touch us all: alcoholism, failed marriages, crippling anxiety, depression, eating disorders, addictions, unemployment, hopelessness, self-harm, abuse. Some people, it seems, move through life relatively unfazed by the volume of heartache around them. Their belief in God's goodness and sovereignty is unshakable. I envy faith like that. But for whatever reason, even as a kid, my faith was fused with doubt. I kept asking why.

As I grew older and continued to learn about who God was, I was both amazed and mystified by him. Like a relentless, twisting vine, doubt and faith grew side by side, merging within me. The two expanded, even flourished together. I began to experience what the Lebanese poet Khalil Gibran once said about doubt, that it "is a pain too lonely to know that faith is his twin brother."[8]

For the most part, the way I responded to doubt was to push it into the margins of my life. I assumed that if I just learned more about God, the Bible, and theology, my doubts would someday be resolved. Boy, was I wrong. Sure, learning helps. But doubt, like faith, is a journey. And a journey is so much more than just memorizing a map or discovering new information about the terrain. It's about walking, feeling, experiencing, moving cautiously forward, and learning to trust. The further you go, the more the sense of mystery grows. And just when you think you've caught a glimpse of God, he covers his face.

I finished high school, then spent a year in Mexico working with orphans who had severe disabilities. As volunteers, we heard stories that were catastrophic. Abuse. Neglect. Rape. One child had cigarette burns all over his body. We all struggled to make sense of it. I remember feeding a boy who couldn't walk, eat, or drink on his own. As I leaned in to give him another bite, his eyes locked on mine, and I could see the pain and frustration he carried. Silently, I tried to pray for him, but didn't know how. The years of suffering he had undergone all seemed so wrong, sadistic, and cruel. I would silently ask, *Why, God? Why do these children have to endure so much?* Broken lives. Broken bodies. Broken minds. And yet, what amazed me is that they still smiled, sang, laughed, and showed me what Jesus looked like.

A few years and several jobs and countries later, I became a pastor in Hawaii. At this point, I had put in some time reading, learning, and studying. As a friend joked, I was a "professional Christian," but my faith wasn't any more immune to doubt. In fact, if anything, it was more vulnerable than ever.

The more I read about God, the more I was struck by how little we actually know about him. Get three theologians in a room, and you'll have four different opinions—and those who are the most opinionated are generally the least loving.

I was stunned and disillusioned when a close spiritual mentor left his wife for another woman.

My wife and I held a grieving mother whose newborn unexpectedly passed away.

Someone I knew committed suicide. Seeking peace, I prayed, but heard nothing.

A friend died in a tragic accident.

Like any who serve in ministry, I felt these stories deeply. Wounds turned to doubt.

Pressing it down, I kept pointing people to what I thought was the answer. Every Sunday I got up on an old wooden stage to share a sermon I had been preparing all week. I opened the Bible and taught, but beneath the words I was struggling to reconcile my growing emotional, theological, and philosophical questions with the God I believed in.

My faith began to feel more and more subdued and fragile. I still believed, but . . .

Augustine wrote:

> You called, shouted, broke through my deafness;
> You flared, blazed, banished my blindness;
> You lavished your fragrance,
> I gasped, and now I pant for you;
> I tasted you, and I hunger and thirst;
> You touched me, and I burned for your peace.[9]

In other words, when you experience God, it changes the way you experience everything else. Sound, sight, smell, breath, hunger, touch; God, like the sun, quickens our senses and illuminates life itself. Faith is the rumor in the country of the blind that there is something more.

I love this poem. I always have.

But I couldn't help but wonder, what about those times when faith in God exposes the shadows too? What happens when you can't reconcile your ideas about God with what you see? What happens when your faith is the reason you're having a hard time believing?

Sometimes I wondered if the Nunez in me was wrong to insist on a world of beauty and hope when the real world seemed so broken.

I kept believing God. I kept teaching people about him. I held on to my faith.

But then, in 2010, the sun went dark. And that's the story I want to share with you next.

Chapter 4

I See Stars

It began when we came to Oxford. Or it began
with shadows of masts and trees. Or it began
with our abandoning our childhood religion: To
believe with certainty, somebody said, one has to
begin by doubting. Wherever it began, what it
was was a coming-together of disparate things.
—Sheldon Vanauken

New life starts in the dark. Whether it is a
seed in the ground, a baby in the womb, or
Jesus in the tomb, it starts in the dark.
—Barbara Brown Taylor

THE ONLY THING HAWAII and England have in common is
that they're islands—and they both have weather that reminds me
of Jesus: the same yesterday, today, and forever. One, however, has
weather that is consistently less gray.

In 2010, my family and I left our church, friends, and the sun of
Hawaii to begin a new life at the University of Oxford in England.

For me, it was a homecoming, a return to the city of my birth. Familiar sights, sounds, and places. But it was more than a return; it was a sojourn into the rugged terrain of doubt. It was a season of testing, stretching, and rethinking. My faith would be challenged in new and painful ways.

For centuries, the city of Oxford has wrestled with questions about God, faith, and doubt. More than nine hundred years ago, the university first began as a nexus of religious study and devotion. The school's motto, *Dominus illuminatio mea*, is taken from the opening words of Psalm 27: "The LORD is my light." As I walked its timeworn, cobblestone streets, I reflected on how many people in Oxford had experienced the power of those words. For example, John Wycliffe, the fourteenth-century professor and Bible translator, used his platform there to call the church to reform, insisting that every Christian should have access to the Bible. Or Hugh Latimer and Nicholas Ridley, who were burnt to death in 1555 for their conviction that this was true. Latimer's last words, as the two men suffered in the city square, were, "Be of good comfort, Master Ridley, and play the man. We shall this day light such a candle, by God's grace, in England, as I trust shall never be put out."[1] Stories like this made moving to Oxford feel as if I was walking on holy ground. The atmosphere was spirited and intense, animated by its deep and tragic history.

Every day I rode my bicycle past the Eagle and Child pub. In the 1930s, C. S. Lewis, who taught at the university, met there with J. R. R. Tolkien and other "Inklings" to discuss theology, literature, and their latest tales of wizards, lions, and hobbits. The mathematician John Lennox once told a class I attended what it was like to sit under C. S. Lewis. He said whenever Lewis taught, the room was pregnant with a sense of anticipation. Students filled the chairs and spilled onto the floor, eagerly waiting for the class to begin. And then, at the exact start time, Lewis charged into the room wearing his Oxford robes. While he hung them up, he launched into his talk. By the time he reached the podium, the lecture was in full stride. He taught without notes, flawlessly, beautifully, and always engaging. Students furiously wrote down what they could. And then, after an hour or more, still teaching, he put his robes back on and walked out the door.

Lennox said it was breathtaking. The atmosphere was vibrant, sparkling with fresh perspectives and ideas.

Almost a century later, a similar ethos still pervaded the university. Virtually everywhere I walked, I heard conversations about God. Some for, many against. Classrooms sprang to life when the topic of God came up. Books lined the shelves of local bookstores. In the pubs, God was on tap. Whenever a public debate took place, it was a packed house.

I've never seen a city so mesmerized by God. And such passionate voices for and against him. During my first year, Stephen Hawking, the late atheist scientist and cosmologist, told *The Guardian*, "There is no heaven or afterlife . . . that is a fairy story for people afraid of the dark."[2] Freud couldn't have said it better. In a speech, John Lennox pushed back: "Atheism is a fairy story for people afraid of the light."[3]

One morning, I listened to a lecture held in a local pub by the scientist, author, and one of the most brilliant men I've ever met, Alister McGrath. Later in the afternoon I ran into Richard Dawkins, who politely asked me for directions to a lecture he was about to teach. We walked the short distance together because I happened to be attending too.

Only in Oxford could you sit in a pub with a theologian in the morning and then walk to class with the world's most famous atheist in the afternoon.

The battle for the soul of Oxford was relentless, and I loved it. But, as the months went by, I faced another battle that was far more personal and unsettling. Doubt, like an ugly cloud, continued to grow inside me. This was partially due to the litany of unresolved questions I had brought with me to Oxford. But it was also a result of the research I was undertaking. As part of my studies that year, I immersed myself in the world of philosophy and atheist writers. I read works by Nietzsche, Sartre, Camus, Harris, Hitchens, and Dennett. I wrote papers about them and their beliefs. I wrestled with their arguments and sought to understand their system of thought.

They articulated historic and philosophical reasons against religious faith.

They professed that suffering disproved the existence of a loving, all-powerful God.

They ridiculed violent and offensive stories in the Bible.

They defended naturalistic explanations for the universe.

They derided religious hope as wish fulfillment.

I could go on.

All of this was in pursuit of a degree. But it was more than that for me. It was an opportunity to honestly reevaluate my beliefs. All of the uncertainty I'd had growing up, the doubts I had suppressed, the tension I'd experienced trying to reconcile my faith with what I had seen, my disillusionment as a pastor, and especially my questions about suffering, suddenly had space to flourish.

The atheist writers gave voice to some of my loneliest questions. They put into words what I had been wrestling with for years. And now, as a full-time graduate student, I had the intellectual breathing room to engage with my struggles. Everything was on the table.

I can't pinpoint when exactly, but during that first year at Oxford, I felt my faith slowly being eclipsed by atheist arguments. The sun grew dark.

Now don't get me wrong. I still loved God. I still prayed. I still went to church. But something was fracturing in my soul. I clung to him, but my grip was weaker. I believed, but I just wasn't sure what that meant anymore. The more I read, the more doubt generated a momentum all on its own. Like a storm, it gathered strength and intensity, disrupting my spirituality, prayer life, and relationship with God. It was unlike anything I'd ever experienced before.

One day, I came across the works of Gary Habermas. He's a keen scholar and thinker and has done groundbreaking research on the resurrection of Jesus. He is a devoted Christian, but he also went through harrowing periods of uncertainty and doubt. His book, *The Thomas Factor*, draws from that story and maps out the terrain of doubt. He suggests there are three types: factual doubt, emotional doubt, and volitional doubt.[4] Factual doubts are related to historical, philosophical, or evidential issues. This could include questions about whether Jesus rose again, the truthfulness of Scripture, or the problem of evil. Emotional doubts arise from our feelings about God. This can be due to some tragedy in our lives, hurt, anxiety, disappointment, or depression. Volitional doubt occurs when the will has chosen to ignore or reject God. The issue here is not lack of evidence but a heart that has willingly chosen not to look for it. I think of Richard Dawkins, who I once heard say there was literally nothing that would persuade him to change his mind about God. Even if God dramatically wrote in the clouds, "I exist," he would write it off as having unknown naturalistic causes. This is a doubt that deliberately chooses unbelief.

Although these three versions of doubt are distinct and have their own root causes and symptoms, they are also deeply interconnected. While in Oxford, I discovered this to be true. Initially, I struggled with factual doubts, as I attempted to understand Christianity in light of probing intellectual questions. But the impact of this was much wider and greater than just an academic exercise: it exposed the longings and fears of my soul. It uncovered weaknesses in how I thought about God. After all the stories of pain I had seen as a missionary and pastor, atheism seemed to offer an intellectual justification to turn away from the faith. And yet, for some reason, I couldn't do it. More than ever, my heart ached for God. I desperately wanted to experience his presence. But in that season, I felt spiritually alone.

My studies took me further into atheism. The words both intrigued and unsettled me. I kept reading. It was like being led to the edge of a cliff. I stepped closer. But the closer I got, the stronger my homesickness for God became.

Nietzsche's words resounded: *If you gaze long into an abyss, the abyss also gazes into you.* I looked down and, at first, saw nothing. But then, as I looked closer, I started to realize it was more than nothing. There was something in the emptiness, a sinister ideology, a nonreality that was dragging life out of me.

I remember pausing midway through a book by Richard Dawkins. He said that we reside in a universe of blind physical forces and genetic replication, and there is "at the bottom no design, no purpose, no evil and no good. Nothing but blind pitiless indifference."[5]

Indifference. Interesting word.

But, I thought, atheism isn't just indifference. It isn't simply a neutral state. It's a system. A worldview. A map. A way to live. Atheism was trying to sell me something. It kept insisting that I take the leap.

I wondered what would happen if I jumped. What lay at the bottom of the abyss? According to Dawkins, no design. No purpose. No evil. No good. But what does that even mean? What kind of reality would that be? Atheism seemed more and more like a black hole: a closed system, self-destructive, and vacuous.

I couldn't shake the question, How would I live if I really believed this were true? What would life look like?

Some atheists have tried to answer that question by suggesting it's up to us to create our own meaning. They claim that truth is subjectively defined, a fabrication of personal and social preferences. An intriguing rebuttal to this comes from an unlikely source: the atheist philosopher John Gray. He argues that relativism is simply a form of humanism, which is itself a diluted form of Christianity. He critiques many atheists for not going far enough. In his book *Straw Dogs*, he maintains that all of our desperate attempts to create meaning are essentially meaningless, morality is without justification, and even the concept of truth is a lie:

> Modern humanism is the faith that through science humankind can know the truth—and so be free. But if Darwin's theory of natural selection is true this is impossible. The human mind serves evolutionary success, not truth. To think otherwise is to resurrect the pre-Darwinian error that humans are different from all other animals.[6]

In other words, according to Gray, we shouldn't even trust our own minds.

Could this be why Nietzsche lost his?

It occurred to me that if everything I was reading about atheism was true, then so much of the human story—our longings, dreams, desires—is fundamentally void of justification. Hope? According to John Gray, "A truly naturalistic view of the world leaves no room for secular hope."[7] Love? It's merely a biochemical reaction. Free will? An illusion. We just dance to our DNA. Justice? A sociological invention without any basis in reality. Morality? In *The Brothers Karamazov*, Dostoyevsky argued that if God doesn't exist, then everything is permitted.[8]

And that is when the abyss started to look exceptionally dark. I began to see that not only is it impossible to truly live like this, but more ominously, it's corrosive to our humanity. The implications of atheism wound us at the deepest level. They're non-human. Anti-human. Parasitic. Ecclesiastes 3:11 says the Divine has "set eternity in the human heart." Yes, we're a conflicted mess of physical impulses—atoms, neurons, muscle, blood, and sweat—but we're more than that too. Purpose thrums in our veins. We're alive. We dream. We aspire for more. We're captured by wonder. We're full of art. We're drawn in by beauty. And, in our best moments, we lay hold of beauty, feel it, taste it, and recreate it. Years ago our ancestors walked away from Eden, and we've been in exile ever since. And yet, something inside of us won't stop languishing for home.

And that's what I couldn't deny. The longing. The nostalgia for home. The abyss of atheism looked more like homelessness. But inwardly, I yearned for God. Knowing him. Loving him. I was thirsty, and nothing but God could satisfy that desire.

>> <<

It was during this time of wrestling that my wonderful wife, Elyssa, urged me to engage the life of the mind with the longings of my heart. She could see I was conflicted. I wasn't sleeping well. I was melancholy, Eeyore-like, and discouraged. I began sacrificing small woodland creatures. Just kidding, it wasn't that bad.

But it was incredibly hard. I was caught between two worlds, and my heart was divided.

"Dominic, what are you reading?" she asked. Usually it was some intense academic work with an uplifting title about the meaninglessness of life or the horrors of a nihilistic universe.

I told her.

She said, "No wonder you're so discouraged! You need to spend time nourishing your mind with truth, beauty, and hope." She challenged me to counterbalance my studies with books that would edify my soul. She encouraged me not to stifle my feelings (one of my many weaknesses) but to open up with people who would care and understand. She urged me to pray. And so, like a wise husband, I did what my wife said.

And it was amazing how those slight, subtle changes began to alter my trajectory.

I picked up the works of C. S. Lewis. I read Christian philosophers like Richard Swinburne, Peter Kreeft, and Alvin Plantinga. I lingered on the insights of scientists like John Polkinghorne and Alister McGrath, people who thought deeply about science but were also deeply committed to faith. I devoured books by theologians such as Augustine, N. T. Wright, and Karl Barth. Barth was especially intimidating. He once said, "I haven't even read everything I wrote!"[9] I revisited my favorite parts of Scripture, beginning with the Gospels.

Something stirred within me.

I was reminded of how rational, sophisticated, and beautiful the Christian faith is.

I realized that God wouldn't die if I ceased to believe in him. But a part of me would.

I found solace in the fact that I wasn't alone in my doubts. Countless men and women have walked that path, too, and yet possessed a rich and vibrant faith.

I discovered that God isn't just found in monochromatic certainties. He's found in a spectrum of beautiful colors, voices, ideas, and shades of gray.

I began to see that faith was less about having everything explained and more about the fragile beauty of trust.

I was more honest with God than I had ever been in my life. I went on long walks and poured out my heart as I shared with him my doubts. He didn't seem upset or surprised, but endlessly accepting. Grace is the experience of infinite belonging. That means there is no abyss so deep that he cannot reach down and save. No faith so broken that he cannot heal. He's with us through it all. Doubt was an entangled, complicated part of who I was (and am), and God is okay with that.

I fell in love with Jesus again.

I had spent years of my life teaching about God, but now I was seeing him with a fresh set of eyes. It was like a burst of sunlight breaking through a storm. God hadn't changed, but I had. I saw things differently.

If home is the life of faith, then doubt is the road we must walk to get there. Of course, there are challenges on the path: pitfalls, loneliness, angst, fear, questions. The word *question* comes from the Latin *quaerere*, which is where we get the word *quest*. A quest, like any adventure, is wrought with obstacles. Every calling has a cost. The mountains are excruciating to climb. The valleys agonizing to endure. For most people, that's what going home looks like. Others I know (and envy) have a much easier time. The journey home is a four-lane highway; hop in the car and you've arrived. Some, like myself, are on the scenic route.

But either way, we're getting there.

And either way, we're not alone.

It dawned on me that what had been wrong in my heart was my relentless quest for certainty. I had come to Oxford with a litany of questions, struggles, and doubts that had accumulated for years. I lost myself in books and study because I was fixated on finding the answers. I was willing to follow the truth wherever it would lead and whatever the cost.

But what I found was that my soul craved far more than just a list of academic explanations. I wanted communion with God. Could this be what Jesus meant when he said, "I am the way"? He didn't say, "I will show you the way." That would be too impersonal and detached, a step removed from intimacy. God doesn't give us a map, he gives us himself. He *is* the way. Just being with him is what our hearts desire.

Recently my daughter asked if we could go to the movies. I didn't hand her the keys and my credit card. Since she's years from getting her license, that wouldn't end well. So, I took her there myself. I am the way to *Star Wars*.

And that's what I needed from God. Not more directions and maps, but closeness, intimacy, and relationship.

I sought certainty but found a God who walked with me all along.

I sought resolution but found relationship.

I sought clarity but found friendship.

He reached out his hand and said, "Follow me."

And when I took his hand, things began to change.

» «

Slowly, painfully, I stepped back from the edge. I continued my studies. The abyss receded. I began the long way home.

And I'm still on the journey.

I wish I could say there was a sudden moment of revelation for me at Oxford: three simple steps that reignited my faith, a Damascus road experience that extricated me from the winter of doubt. But there wasn't. It was far less dramatic and much more of a process.

It's like the scene in C. S. Lewis's *The Lion, the Witch and the Wardrobe*, when Lucy, Peter, and Susan stumbled through a closet into a strange world. Narnia was bleak, frigid, and under the spell of a white witch. But then they met Mr. and Mrs. Beaver, who talked to them in hushed tones of a great lion named Aslan who would someday make things right again. They heard excited whispers in the woods that he was on the move. They didn't see him, but they soon saw signs of him. The snow started to melt. The ice began to thaw. The river broke through its frozen shell. Hints of spring, the dawn of a new age. The birds inaugurated his arrival with song.

That's the best way I can describe what happened in Oxford. It felt like the spell of winter slowly, gradually faded into spring.

And if I'm honest, that's where I am today. My soul feels much more alive, but there are still moments when the wind is biting cold. Patches of snow lay scattered on the ground. God is still a mystery to me. He's a closer friend, but there is still so much I don't understand. I have questions. I still ask why. I still struggle with doubt. My heart resonates with the words of theologian and pastor Christopher Wright:

> It seems to me that the older I get the less I think I really understand God. Which is not to say that I don't love and trust him. On the contrary, as life goes on, my love and trust grow deeper, but my struggle with what God does or allows grows deeper too.[10]

Every day, I'm leaning into the truth of those words. God doesn't demand that we understand him, but he does ask us to trust him.

That's why I'm so thankful for that season in Oxford. It was disorienting and challenging, but it taught me to trust. It reawakened my longing for God. It broke and restored me. It taught me lessons I'll never forget.

First of all, I'm convinced that times of doubt are not something to endure alone. I am so thankful for the support and counsel of my wife and others who prayed for me during that time. The books helped, but there is nothing like the synergy and beautiful authenticity community provides. We'll unpack that more (along with other practical advice) in chapters 9–11.

Secondly, while some forms of doubt are potentially devastating (especially emotional doubts), other doubts are overrated. I once met someone who said they lost their faith because they read a book that challenged their view on hell. *Really?* That may be interesting to discuss, but it's not worth losing your faith over.

Did you know that a city block of fog, which when you're in it can seem so dense, is only equivalent to half a cup of water? That's incredible. A few sips of water can swallow up a city! Doubt can work the same way. The actual issue may or may not be that significant, but it wants to be. Left unchecked it can get blown up in our mind and distort our perspective of God. It thirsts to be bigger than it actually is. Unhealthy doubt is the ultimate drama queen, refusing to be resolved, relentlessly deconstructing, demanding to be the center of attention. And so we have to put it in check, see it for what it is, and get it back in the glass. Again, more on what this looks like when we arrive at the closing chapters of the book.

Thirdly, I came to see that doubt isn't the rival of faith. In fact, you could argue that doubt depends upon faith for its existence. When you doubt something, it's only because you first believed. You can believe without doubting, but you can't doubt without believing. Every doubt has a foundation that it's standing on. So, for example, if you believe that suffering disproves the existence of God, your underlying belief is that the world shouldn't be that way. But here's the paradox: a world without God is a world that doesn't care about suffering. It's just how naturalism works. So, your doubt about God is, in reality, a stronger belief that he does, or at least ought to, exist. You then have to grapple with the kind of God he is. Do you see what's happened? Your doubt has led you into a penetrating quest for truth.

If you follow your doubts to your beliefs, you may be surprised where it leads you. And you may also be surprised by the depth it can bring to your faith. Like a painting, it's the shadows and shades of gray that add balance, contrast, and beauty. Doubt is the shadow of faith; it's the contrast that makes the art come alive. And it's the contrast of being far from home that makes coming home so meaningful.

Which leads me to my final point, and where I want to spend a little more time. My study of atheism revealed its dirty secret: it is a faith position too. Atheist and philosopher Thomas Nagel writes,

> I want atheism to be true and am made uneasy by the fact that some of the most intelligent and well-informed people I know are religious believers. It isn't just that I don't believe in God and, naturally, hope that I'm right in my belief. It's that I hope there is no God! I don't want there to be a God; I don't want the universe to be like that.[11]

That kind of honesty is so refreshing—and rare. Nagel admits his atheism is a hope, a belief, a chosen way of seeing the universe. Far from being a logical outcome, or an inevitable answer due to the surplus of evidence, atheism is something that must be taken on faith.

Of course, this is true of any worldview. Whether it's atheism, agnosticism, deism, pantheism, animism, or Christianity, it all demands a leap into the unknown. Now, I do believe the leap makes more sense in the direction of Christianity, but even then, I still hope God will catch me on the other side.

But if it's all a leap of faith, then why jump? Why not stay still? Can't we all be agnostic? The problem is, life doesn't work that way. Life wrenches us out of our passivity, forces us to choose, and demands we engage with its wonder, chaos, tragedy, heartache, and pain. To live is to interact with the world. To be human is to believe. To be human is to doubt.

And that means atheists doubt too.

The Christian wonders, *God, are you really there? Do you have a purpose for my life? Is there an afterlife?*

The atheist likewise wonders, *Is God really not there? Is there a purpose for my life? What if there is an afterlife?*

We all live in the tension of uncertainty. We all breathe the second-hand smoke of doubt. That's a fact. But the question we still have to answer is how shall we live? How will we step into the unknown?

Personally, I choose to trust God. And I'm doing my best to follow the way of Jesus. It's often hard, unsettling, and confusing, but it's also mesmerizing, breathtaking, and full of joy. Dale Carnegie once wrote, "Two men looked out from prison bars. One saw the mud, the other saw stars."[12]

I see them too. And there's nothing like it.

And if it's all wrong? If God is a fantasy? If death is the end? So be it.

According to the sixteenth century mathematician Blaise Pascal,

Belief is a wise wager. Granted that faith cannot be proved, what harm will come to you if you gamble on its truth and it proves false? If you gain, you gain all; if you lose, you lose nothing.[13]

Well said. But I think this is about so much more than pragmatics. Belief in God is not just what you gain or lose after death, it's about how you live now.

I recently read a powerful true story about the time war was breaking out in Sarajevo.[14] The year was 1992 and bombs were falling throughout the country, decimating towns, businesses, and lives. On May 27, a bomb fell on a bakery, killing twenty-two people. It just so happened that the cellist from the Sarajevo Opera, Vedran Smajlovic, lived nearby. He heard the explosion and rushed outside. Bodies, blood, and fractured pieces of the building were scattered everywhere. Smajlovic was devastated but decided to fight back in the only way he knew how: music. For twenty-two days, a day for each victim, he carried his cello to the scorched site of the bombing, sat on a chair, and played.

In a place of ruin, his songs became a symbol of renewal. In the confusion and tragedy of war, an anthem of peace. Victims of that conflict, not only in Sarajevo, but throughout the world, were reminded that beauty could be born in broken places.

Our world is like that bombed-out bakery. We're confused and lonely, stretching frantically through the rubble in search of purpose. We're handed two scripts. One says there is no meaning. It's all an accident. Things happen. And by the way, you're an accident too.

But Jesus gives us another script. He says that life does have meaning. And everything about who you are, the breath in your lungs, the heart pounding in your chest, your tears, fears, and dreams, matter. He promises that justice will reign, mercy will triumph, what's ruined will be rebuilt; and he invites us to join him the best we know how.

Some say this is nothing more than a fantasy. And, who knows, maybe they're right. Maybe we are the crazy, deluded ones. But I would rather live my life in hope, searching for a beautiful God, than in the ache and emptiness of a godless world.

I believe there is more to existence than blind, pitiless indifference.

I believe in a God who created us, loved us, gave himself for us, and is drawing us relentlessly, inexorably, lovingly, to himself.

I believe life has purpose.

I believe death does not have the last word.

I believe in ultimate reality and, like Nunez's valley, it is teeming with life, beauty, color, and depth.

I believe doubt is sacramental. It breaks us, wounds us, but then—if we let it—brings us back to life.

I believe even when the sun goes dark, it will return again. The eclipse will pass. The world may look different, but so will we.

And I believe there is more to us than matter. Where some see mud . . .

I see stars.

Part II

Exploring the Terrain:

*Finding Hope in Life's
Hardest Questions*

Chapter 5

Can I Trust the Bible?

The Bible is alive, it speaks to me;
it has feet, it runs after me;
it has hands, it lays hold of me.
—MARTIN LUTHER

In a nutshell, the Bible from Genesis 3 to
Revelation 22 tells the story of a God reckless
with desire to get his family back.
—PHILIP YANCEY

IF OUR FAITH IS going to thrive, it will often require a journey
deep into doubt. Doubt's greatest strength is secrecy. It loves to
linger just beneath the surface of our lives. But if we name our
doubts and drag them into the light, we may find resolution, or
we may discover the tension of authentically living a doubt-filled
faith. Either way, it's not until we engage our doubts that our faith
can grow.

So let's name and unpack some of the specific issues that fuel doubt in our lives, beginning with Scripture. The Bible is the bed-rock of our faith, and yet, for some people, the cause of so many doubts. Let's face it. It is a complex, mysterious, beautiful, and often bewildering book. It can impart life-giving vision, but the challenges it raises can also obscure and cloud our faith.

Have you ever experienced that? I know I have. As a pastor, my world is the Bible. Every week I read it, study it, pull it apart, and try to put it back together for people to understand on Sunday. I love it. But, if I'm honest, there are times when the Bible creates more confusion than clarity.

I recently sat down with someone, and for him this was the issue.

"Dominic," he stammered, "I think I've lost my faith in God." His eyes were moist with tears, his voice stinging with passion. I could tell he meant every word he said. He was raised in a Christian home, sat in church every weekend, read his Bible, even went to a Christian school. Now, in his early twenties, he was wondering if any of it was true.

At one point I must have mentioned a verse in the Bible, because he said, "I guess that's the problem. I just don't believe in that book anymore." He had all kinds of reasons why: too bloody, archaic, controversial, contradictory, politically incorrect. As he spoke, his voice got louder and louder. People in the coffee shop nervously tried to avoid eye contact. And then he hesitated. Putting down his cup, he whispered, "Right now I have so many questions, so many doubts about his Word . . . I don't know if I can trust him anymore."

I've had so many conversations like this. Maybe you have too. People struggling, doubting, confused by the very thing that is supposed to strengthen our faith: the Bible.

So how do we engage this issue? Where do we begin?

Well, let's step back a moment and talk about what the Bible is. This is important because we often lose the forest for the trees; we get so hung up on chapter and verse that we fail to appreciate its astonishing beauty and power. Regardless of where you're at on the spectrum of faith, one thing we can all agree on is that the Bible is the most influential, life-changing book in the history of the world. There is no other book like it. It has shaped cultures, reformed nations, inspired poets, and affected the flow and fate of history. People have lived, bled, and died for it. Its influence is absolutely staggering. The Bible is the bestselling book of all time, selling twenty-five million copies each year. It has been translated into more than 2,200 languages and has bridged the gap between ethnic groups, politics, cultures, and civilizations.

One reason for its universal impact is its diversity. It was written over a period of 1,500 years on three different continents in three different languages: Hebrew, Aramaic, and Greek. The authors came from a variety of backgrounds and vocations: farmers, shepherds, poets, fishermen, politicians, priests. Together they wrote sixty-six different books in a dazzling array of literary genres: law, history, poetry, letters, gospels, prophecy, and wisdom literature.

What's remarkable, however, is that in spite of its diversity, the Bible is still unified in its overarching narrative of redemption. From beginning to end, it's all about a God never giving up on his people.

That simple idea has captivated countless lives. The existential philosopher Immanuel Kant praised the Bible, calling it "The greatest benefit which the human race has ever experienced."[1] Martin Luther King Jr., who was moved by its empowering message to champion the cause of racial justice, maintained that it was full of "many profound truths which one cannot escape."[2] Even the social activist Gandhi, who was Hindu, said,

> You Christians look after a document containing enough dyna-
> mite to blow all civilization to pieces, turn the world upside
> down and bring peace to a battle-torn planet. But you treat it as
> though it is nothing more than a piece of literature.[3]

Wow. And ouch.

But he's right. The book that we often neglect and leave sitting on a shelf is brimming with untapped potential to dynamically change the world.

It already has.

When you look at the innumerable aspects of our world that the Bible has influenced, it's breathtaking. For example, consider language. Did you know that the Bible is quoted more often than any other piece of literature in history? Words and phrases that we use every day find their source in the Bible. The idiom "a drop in the bucket" comes from Isaiah 40:15. "The powers that be" is Romans 13:1. A "broken heart" goes back three thousand years to Psalm 34:18. Even "you made me do it," which sounds like Taylor Swift, is actually the apostle Paul (2 Corinthians 12:11 CEB). And there are so many more examples.

In the arts, the Bible's influence is everywhere. Poetry, liter-ature, paintings, sculptures, movies, music, and songs are soaked in biblical stories, themes, and theology. For centuries Christians, inspired by Scripture, were pioneers in imagining and creating beauty. To them, the Bible wasn't just a flat, two-dimensional book. It came alive. It stirred, breathed, and drew them in. It danced on the pages.

The Bible has a way of sweeping other stories into its story. Classics such as *The Grapes of Wrath*, *The Scarlet Letter*, *Macbeth*, *Moby Dick*, *Paradise Lost*, and *The Brothers Karamazov* are filled with Scripture. And it's not just direct quotations or references; it's an atmosphere of Scripture that saturates these works. They relentlessly engage with questions that the Bible asks and assume a degree of biblical literacy among their readers.

If you take a stab at reading a good book, chances are it will bleed Scripture.

The Bible's imprint on the world is undeniable. No wonder Jesus said, "Heaven and earth will pass away, but my words will never pass away" (Matthew 24:35). The Bible has stood the test of time, transformed the face of culture, and flourished through adversity. In the words of Indian scholar Vishal Mangalwadi, it is "the book that made your world."[4]

Now, I think most of us agree with this. But here's the tension. While we acknowledge the impact the Bible has had, we are conflicted by what it says. We pay lip service to the Bible, but we don't trust it. We acknowledge its shaping power. We're just not sure if it should be a shaping force for our lives.

Gallup has conducted research in which they discovered that 26 percent of Americans view the Bible critically, as "a book of fables, legends, history and moral precepts recorded by man."[5] Only 24 percent of Americans believe the Bible is the literal Word of God. What is significant about this poll is this is the first time in Gallup's history that skeptics of the Bible have surpassed its believers. For some reason, doubt about the Bible is on the rise.

Why is this?

A lot of factors feed into this narrative. We could talk about cultural trends and the shifting ethos of our culture. We live in a time when those who value Scripture are often pushed to the margins, ridiculed, or shamed.

We could talk about the role of technology and its power to distract us from sustained, linear thinking. As a result of our Googled brains, we don't read as much as we used to.[6] It's hard to take Scripture seriously if we don't know what it says. In his book *Religious Literacy*, Stephen Prothero argues,

> The disparity between Americans' veneration of the Bible and their understanding of it, paint[s] a picture of a nation that believes God has spoken in Scripture but can't be bothered to listen to what God has to say.[7]

It turns out the Bible is the bestselling book that nobody has ever read.

Another possible cause emerges from our biases in education. It's tragic how many institutions buy into a script that either ignores, vilifies, or intentionally deconstructs Scripture. I think of the many students I've met with, some raised in Christian homes, who sat through their first literature class in college, were told the Bible is primitive and barbaric, and returned home with their faith in pieces.

For those still trying to believe, these factors have created a virulent social environment. Trust toward Scripture has given way to suspicion, reverence to ridicule. And, to make matters worse, when we actually dust off the pages of the Bible to read it for ourselves, we are confronted with stories and doctrines that are confusing, weird, or even offensive.

How many read-through-the-Bible-in-a-year plans have died the death of Leviticus? Genesis is interesting. Exodus is mostly fast moving, and if you don't like it, you can always watch the movie. But Leviticus?

"Ye shall not round the corners of your heads" (Leviticus 19:27 KJV).

There goes your bowl haircut.

And then there's all the blood, sacrifices, and endless lists of archaic rules.

Some persevere to Deuteronomy, only to read, "Do not cook a young goat in its mother's milk" (14:21). You're like, "Dang it," take the goat off the stove and put it back outside.

If you keep going, the stories get darker. Joshua and Judges are packed with accounts of war, violence, slaughter, greed, and rape. Second Kings has a story about children making fun of the prophet Elisha. He cursed them, then bears lumbered out of the woods and tore them apart. Try teaching *that* in Sunday school.

We could go on. Mark Twain said, "It ain't the parts of the Bible that I can't understand that bother me, it's the parts that I do understand."[8]

Many of us can relate.

Of course, struggling to understand God's Word is nothing new. Genesis tells us that even Adam and Eve, living in a God-drenched garden, were confronted by similar doubts: "Did God really say?" (Genesis 3:1). These words slid into their hearts, sabotaging their confidence in God. Years later, and miles away from Eden, the question lingers in our hearts too.

Because so much of what we believe about God—our theology, practices, and understanding of how the world works—is derived from Scripture, when we question it, we question everything. Like a worn-out, tattered sweater, a single string can unravel it all. And pretty soon what we have left is a barely read, seldom relevant, dusty old book. Or just another ancient document, changed too many times to count. Or a sappy collection of self-help tales designed to teach us a moral lesson. Like *Aesop's Fables* or Dr. Seuss. Mother Goose meets Jesus.

But is that all the Bible is? Myth? Fable? A book of unreliable, made-up stories that no one can trust?

The answer is an overwhelming, emphatic no.

The Bible is the most reliable piece of ancient literature in existence. It's not just a randomly written book, carelessly maintained and passed around. Rather, its legacy is one of unrivaled historic integrity. An extraordinary example of this came on the heels of World War II, when a group of Bedouin shepherds and archaeologists discovered the Dead Sea Scrolls in Israel. The scrolls ranged in age from 250 BC to AD 50, and many skeptics assumed that once they were compared with more recent manuscripts, they would prove the Bible's inaccuracy. They were astonished, however, by how meticulously preserved the manuscripts were.[9] Old Testament scribes, fervently committed to its authority, had copied each word, each letter, with stunning precision and accuracy.

The same can be said for the New Testament. Outside of the Bible, the *Iliad* and *Odyssey*, with 2,500 manuscripts, are the most well-preserved documents we have. That's remarkable when you consider that Homer wrote them nearly three thousand years ago. And yet, the New Testament has more than *ten times* this number. It is, by far, the most accurate and trustworthy ancient document in the world. According to Clark Pinnock,

> There exists no document from the ancient world witnessed by so excellent a set of textual and historical testimonies and offering so superb an array of historical data on which an intelligent

decision may be made. An honest [person] cannot dismiss a source of this kind.[10]

Now, the fact that there are tens of thousands of documents validating the Bible doesn't mean that we have to trust it personally, but at the very least, we can trust it historically.

>> <<

For many people, however, the issue isn't how the stories of the Bible were preserved; it's what the stories of the Bible actually say. Let's face it, if parts of the book of Judges were put on film, an R-rating wouldn't go far enough. How can we trust the Bible when it's so graphic and disturbing?

This is what we need to know:

The Bible is brutally honest about the human story. It's awkward, messy, and weird. Why? Because people are awkward, messy, and weird. So, of course there is scandal, adultery, sexism, violence, and war. Because that's what people *do*. The Bible is true to life. It doesn't gloss over our imperfections. Nor is it just a book of abstract philosophical ideas. It confronts us in the mud and mess of life. It's about real people with real issues, insecurities, weaknesses, and flaws.

Yet, just because the Bible honestly records the stories of real people, it doesn't mean that God endorses what they did. For example, in Genesis, God created male and female in his image as his ideal for marriage. One man, one woman, for one lifetime. Polygamy, polyamory, adultery, and "open" relationships were all off the table. God made Adam and Eve, not Adam, Eve, Lucy, and Jane. But it didn't take long for humanity to radically change the script.

Only a few pages later, a man named Lamech married two women (Genesis 4). Later, Abraham, Jacob, David, and Solomon all had multiple wives. This was never God's original design for marriage, and, if you look closely at their stories, they always end in heartache.

When the Bible describes the destructive choices individuals made, it's not giving us a map to follow but a lesson to learn. God is trying to teach us something. In some cases, God directly tells us what the lesson is (for instance, when Nathan confronted David after his affair in 2 Samuel 12), but there are many times when he does not. God's silence here does not mean approval but rather an invitation for us to go deeper, process, and ask questions about the story. God gave people complete, and sometimes dangerous, freedom to forge their own path, even if it led them away from him. We need to discern between what God allows and what he approves.

That is why it's vital we ask hermeneutical, big-picture questions, such as "When I look at the Bible as a whole, what is God's heart toward this moral issue?" And, "In light of the overriding theme of redemption, how should I understand what happened?" A good litmus test is Jesus. In Matthew 5:17, he said that he was the fulfillment of the law. In other words, Jesus shows us what the story means. When the Bible records something that seems morally ambiguous or offensive, Jesus is our interpretive lens to decipher the heart of God.

Another key to discerning God's heart in Scripture is by having a clear understanding of the word *inspired*. Second Timothy 3:16 says that "every scripture is inspired by God" (CEB). Many Christians have interpreted this as: "The Bible is God's Word; therefore, every word is automatically his will for your life." I remember believing this growing up. I would even open the Bible randomly, expecting a verse to speak to me in my precise situation. Some days it worked.

Some days it didn't. Then, one day, I opened to Mark 14:52: "He fled naked, leaving his garment behind." It made me uncomfortable even reading it. The first streaker in the Bible. I'm so glad I interpreted this as history, not command. And so are my neighbors.

So what does it mean when we say the Bible is "inspired"? Simply this: God moved the human authors, through their unique personalities and cultural contexts, to receive and communicate truth to the world.

That is why the Bible isn't afraid to tell us who we are. It tells the truth. The good, the bad, and the ugly. And it tells these stories out of diverse countries, cultures, contexts, and people. This is important: the Bible is the Word of God, but it is also the product of humans who penned the words. It was written by actual people, in actual places and times. This isn't a secret. The Bible itself reminds us of its human influence. Consider a few examples:

- "Moses wrote down this law and gave it to the Levitical priests." (Deuteronomy 31:9)
- "While Jeremiah dictated all the words the LORD had spoken to him, Baruch wrote them on the scroll." (Jeremiah 36:4)
- "To the rest I say this (I, not the Lord) . . ." (1 Corinthians 7:12)

Moses, Jeremiah, and Paul all had a part to play in creating Scripture. They were ordinary, flawed men God used as vehicles to communicate truth. They spoke for him. But, in the process, God didn't erase their individual styles, personalities, passions, or intellect.

Like Jesus, the Bible is both human *and* divine. "The Word

became flesh and dwelt among us" (John 1:14 NKJV). It's both-and. It comes to us and it dwells among us. It speaks to us and it speaks for us. It convicts us and it reflects us. It is higher than us and it understands us. To read the Bible, then, is to encounter both the heartbeat of God and our own.

That is what we mean when we say it's inspired.

It's not a magic book that fell from the sky.

It's not a cosmic fortune cookie that we break open for airy platitudes.

It's not even a handbook of readily accessible answers.

The Bible is an ancient library of sixty-six books, written in different languages, genres, and cultures, but together it tells a unified story that leads to Jesus.

The implications of this are huge.

At the top of the list, it means we have to recognize the radical dissimilarity between our world and the world in which it was written. Every time we open it, we are opening a chasm of cultures. And it doesn't take long to realize that they had values, traditions, and ways of life that look nothing like our own. According to E. Randolph Richards,

> We can easily forget that Scripture is a foreign land and that reading the Bible is a cross-cultural experience. To open the Word of God is to step into a strange world where things are very unlike our own. Most of us don't speak the languages. We don't know the geography or the customs or what behaviors are considered rude or polite.[11]

If you've done much travel, you know what it's like to step into a strange world. Not long ago I took a trip to Dubai and went on a camel safari. I rode for several hours in the hot desert sun, swatting flies, wiping sweat from my face, and sitting lopsided on the back of a very lumpy (and grumpy) camel. Honestly, it was a little overrated. When we were finished, we huddled around a fire with a group of locals. They told us stories of Arabian nights and epic conquests. It was so nomadic, rustic, Bedouin. Then they served us food. It tasted a little odd, but, not wanting to be rude, I ate every bite. We then washed it down with a cup of unusually sweet, strange milk. I finally mustered the courage to ask what I had just imbibed. Camel milk. I didn't know that was possible, but they weren't kidding. (I wouldn't be surprised if that someday becomes a thing in progressive cities. Organic, cage-free, gluten-free camel milk.) And the food? One of the men laughed, "Oh, that was camel meat."

In a single night I rode a camel, ate a camel, and drank a camel. The only thing I didn't do was smoke a camel. But after hearing about my dinner, part of me wished I could!

Cultures stretch us, challenge us, and give us new ways of looking at the world. The same is true with the Bible. It's the ultimate desert safari. It surprises, shocks, and reframes our presuppositions. And so much of it is dissimilar from the world in which we live: food, marriage, music, family, warfare, ethics, honor, politics. If we're to make any sense of this at all, we need to do the heavy lifting of peeling back the layers of history, culture, and time. We need to ask questions. We need to investigate, explore, discover.

Reading the Bible well demands that we make an investment. We have to work hard. This is where good commentaries, books, dictionaries, and concordances are so invaluable. I can't tell you how many times I've come across a weird verse, spent a little effort digging beneath the surface, and seen the issue resolved. For example, I remember being confused by the Old Testament story of Ruth sneaking up to Boaz and laying at his feet while he slept (Ruth 3:7). I can only imagine what went through Boaz's mind when he woke up. Groggy surprise blended with panicked reflection on what he'd had to drink the night before. But as I studied the passage more and did my best to understand the culture, I discovered that laying at someone's feet was essentially a way to propose marriage. In other words, Ruth was saying, "You've got cold feet, Boaz, so let me help you out. I'll make the first move."

Grasping the context and culture of the Bible takes time. It wasn't written just to give us quick, scripted answers to life's problems. Nor does it welcome spiritual gold diggers—people who just want the upgrade but don't care about the relationship. The Bible, like anything worthwhile, demands authenticity and investment. Like a tender and thriving friendship, we can't rush it. We have to wrestle, weep, struggle, laugh, cry, think, and invest. Eugene Peterson, in his deliciously titled work *Eat This Book*, wrote, "Reading is an immense gift, but only if the words are assimilated, taken into the soul—eaten, chewed, gnawed, received in unhurried delight."[12]

He's not saying we have to lock ourselves in a room for years with a stack of expensive commentaries and resources to benefit from the words. Plenty of people I know have all of that, along with more academic degrees than a thermometer, but remain indifferent toward God. It's one thing to know the Bible but another thing to know the one who inspired it. The Bible isn't just about information; it's about formation. And if your heart is open, it will speak to you now.

» «

When I read the Bible in my season of doubt, one of the things that struck me was how much I could relate not only to its humanness but also to the angst and untamed rawness of its cast of characters. Virtually every time I opened its pages, I was confronted by the realization that I wasn't alone. Story after story brought to life their painful collisions with doubt.

Abraham and Sarah doubted God's promise (Genesis 17:17–22; 18:10–15). Gideon doubted his calling (Judges 6:36). Job doubted God's character (Job 7:20–21). John the Baptist, whom Jesus called "the greatest of all the prophets," doubted if Jesus was the Messiah (Matthew 11:1–6). Peter doubted his faith (Mark 14:66–72). Thomas doubted the resurrection (John 20:24–29). The list goes on. Scripture doesn't edit out the stories of those who struggled to believe. It weaves their heart-rending struggles into the narrative. The highs and lows, faith's ebbs and flows, are endlessly brought to life.

David, Israel's king, hero, warrior, and songwriter was, at times, overcome with doubt. Read the Psalms. He struggled deeply. His heart bled. His voice was hoarse from his shouts. He questioned. Wept. And yet, he still sang his song.

That is what I love about the Bible: Its doubters are its authors. Its detractors are its advocates. They were bewildered, perplexed, and often unsure. Yet they figured out a way to flourish in the tension of an imperfect faith.

And God was okay with that. Not only okay, but he gave them the biggest platform the world has ever known.

What this means for us is that if you're doubting the Bible, the best thing you can do is read the Bible. It gives your doubts a place of belonging. It articulates your struggle. Far from being preached at, you'll join myriad sojourners who have been in your shoes. Or sandals. They know what it's like. They've experienced times when the sun went dark. Their feet have slipped too.

But somehow, they kept believing. They worshipped, they sang, they wrote. They found delight in the God they doubted. They didn't understand him, but they loved him.

That's why I can't stop reading their words. They're real. They're true. They're beautiful. They radiate life and possibility.

But ultimately what I love about the Bible is that it brings me closer to Jesus.

In Luke 24 Jesus appeared to his doubt-filled disciples on the Emmaus road. Their hearts were heavy because their Messiah had been savagely tortured on a Roman cross. The story didn't end how they'd expected. Their leader was gone; their hope for a new world extinguished.

But it was there, on that dusty road, that Jesus met them. As they walked, he walked by their side. Somehow, they didn't recognize him. Something about his resurrected body, perhaps? Or maybe their eyes were clouded by grief. They had assumptions about how the world worked, and resurrection wasn't part of it. The air was thick with irony. They walked, talked, discussed. And then, Jesus opened the Scriptures—and told them how all of it spoke of him.

All of it.

At that moment their hearts "burned" within them (v. 32), their eyes were opened, and they saw Jesus.

Many of us, like the weary, mystified disciples, are on the Emmaus road. We want to believe but can't get past our presuppositions and doubt. We're so distracted by the Bible's ubiquitous cultural weirdness that we fail to notice the One who is walking by our side. We fixate on the blood, the death, the cross, and may have missed the most important detail of all: resurrection and an old tomb erupting in new life. The Bible wasn't written to pacify and lull us to sleep with theoretical, abstract phrases and lofty ideas but to meet us where we're at. Here. In the real world. It's therefore unafraid to engage with the brokenness of our story, sometimes alarmingly so. But then it points us to how the story ends: the renewal of all things.

The Bible unsettles us, offends us, and then it sets us free.

It ruthlessly deconstructs our idea of what a holy book should look like; it's shocking, scandalous, enraging, flagrantly putting on display the catastrophic effects of sin. But if we keep turning the pages, we'll fall in love with a God of extravagant healing and grace.

"But what about all the sex and violence?" (complains the culture that created *Game of Thrones!*) There's one big difference: while our culture glorifies violence, capitalizes on injustice, and advocates twisted sexuality, the Bible pushes back on it and leads us to Jesus. The Bible doesn't end with violent Old Testament wars, a litany of obscure commands, or scandalous sex scenes. It ends when heaven crashes into earth and Jesus' presence fills and resurrects the earth.

The Bible is all about Jesus. So, when we read it, we're not just reading a book of history or prophecy; we're encountering the God who is with us now. Jesus is on every page. He is the focus, purpose, and trajectory. He is the hope, promise, and fulfillment. And not only is this book all about him; Jesus himself was ceaselessly passionate about it. He read the Bible, studied the Bible, memorized the Bible, quoted from the Bible, taught from the Bible. According to Philip Yancey,

> It is the Bible Jesus read. He traced in its passages every important fact about himself and his mission . . . These are the prayers

Jesus prayed, the poems he memorized, the songs he sang, the bedtime stories he heard as a child, the prophecies he pondered.[13]

I can't help but wonder if we've been looking at the Bible the wrong way. Maybe we've been so obsessed with how an ancient book resolves all of our historical, cultural, scientific, and moral questions that doubt has become inevitable. But what if its primary objective isn't intellectual certainty but to lead us into a flourishing relationship with God? The Bible is meant to be *lived*, not controlled.

Maybe we need to see the Bible less through modern eyes (How is it rational?) or postmodern eyes (How does it speak to me?). Maybe we need to accept it for what it is: an eccentric, weird, difficult, challenging, inspiring, inviting, paradigm-disrupting book that, page by page, story by story, culminates in the person of Jesus.

And if that's true, then like any relationship, it takes time. We need perseverance to dig past its ancient, crusty surface and so uncover truth. And we need a ton of humility to reorient our thinking when that happens.

Either way, I find peace in knowing that its authors were also its doubters. They struggled too. But they continued walking the Emmaus road, because they believed that in the end it was all worth it. They had hope that someday, somehow, they would see their Messiah. And that's what makes the Bible not only something to trust, but something to live by.

Chapter 6

Is Science the Enemy of Faith?

Science without religion is lame;
religion without science is blind.
—Albert Einstein

Two things fill the mind with ever new and
increasing admiration and awe . . . the starry
heavens above and the moral law within.
—Immanuel Kant

IT WAS MORE THAN four hundred years ago that Francis Bacon, now recognized as the architect of the scientific method, made the claim that God has given us two books to study: Scripture and creation. God's Word and God's world. He believed that not only was there a beautiful synthesis between them, but that they, in different ways, give us a fuller revelation of who God is.

The idea that God reveals himself through more than just the

Bible isn't new. In the book of Psalms, David wrote, "The heavens declare the glory of God; the skies proclaim the work of his hands" (Psalm 19:1). In Romans, Paul said the wonders of the physical world are evidence God exists:

> For since the creation of the world God's invisible qualities—his eternal power and divine nature—have been clearly seen, being understood from what has been made, so that people are without excuse. (Romans 1:20)

For thousands of years, believers found joy in creation, stood in awe of its beauty, and delighted in what God had made. Adam's first job was to name the animals. Job relished in God's creative genius: "The wings of the ostrich flap joyfully" (Job 39:13). Jesus often used nature in his parables, holding it up as a prism to animate our understanding of the kingdom of God. Monasteries in the Middle Ages became centers for scientific innovation. Cathedrals were designed not only as places of worship but as astronomical observatories. Pastors in pre-Enlightenment Europe used to spend time, as part of their job, studying nature and weaving their discoveries into their sermons.

Whether from gazing at the Milky Way at night or examining the vibrant world living in a handful of dirt, believers allowed science to enrich their understanding of the world and enlarge their love for the God who spoke it into existence. Rather than being competitors in a battle of worldviews, faith and science were once seen as partners in joyous, theological discovery.

How times have changed.

» «

During the ninth season of *The Simpsons*, Lisa found a fossil on an archaeological dig with her class. Some who were religious insisted the bones were from a deceased angel, but Lisa was unconvinced. The controversy ultimately led to a riot, violence, and a court order requiring the angry mob to keep a safe distance away so that science could proceed. Turns out it wasn't an angel after all but a creative publicity stunt for a local mall. And it worked.

The episode ended with a vigorous shopping spree.[1] Yay for science.

For many of us, it's a familiar narrative:

Religion stands in the way of science. Science moves us forward.

Religion is unpredictable. Science is methodical.

Religion sees the divine in everything. Science looks for the facts.

Religion and science are at war.

Historians call this "the conflict thesis." To understand some of its history, let's go back three hundred years.

In the 1700s Europe was undergoing a seismic shift in its understanding of the world. Enlightenment ideas, marked by a sharpening cynicism toward authority and superstition, pushed back on theology. The scientific revolution shattered popular views of cosmology. People began to question the role of religion. Increasingly, the church and all it stood for was perceived as an enemy of progress, a relic of a bygone era. The French philosopher Jean d'Alembert argued that civilization needed to renounce the church and embrace rationalism and scientific thought. His words were eagerly embraced by a public that was disenchanted with religion—its wars, politics, scandals, and control. A few years later, the historian Andrew Dickson White declared that science was gradually displacing religion and would soon usher in a new and progressive age. Until then, he said, "The conflict between two epochs in the evolution of human thought: the theological and the scientific"[2] would continue to rage.

These ideas scorched their way into European thought and consciousness. Enlightenment thinkers disputed cherished beliefs. The historicity of Adam and Eve. Noah's flood. The authenticity of Scripture. The resurrection of Jesus. Nothing was sacred. Descartes even questioned reality itself, before concluding that the basis of reality begins with our minds: *Cogito ergo sum.* I think, therefore I am.

The rift between science and faith grew.

Then in 1859, Charles Darwin, who at one point had studied to be a vicar in the Church of England, published his theory of evolution. This changed everything. Although Darwin didn't intend it to be a polemic against Christianity, many, understandably, took it that way. Darwinism quickly spread beyond the domain of science, influencing the worlds of philosophy, psychology, theology, education, and sociology. Some even used his words as a justification for racism, colonialism, and genocide.

Such is the power of an idea.

As evolutionary theory, scientific discoveries, and Enlightenment philosophy gained traction, it fueled the belief that religion was standing in the way of progress. At least, that's how some people took it.

Which brings us to twenty-first-century America.

After becoming a Christian in middle school, I remember being fed versions of this conflict narrative. It was usually in small doses: a well-meaning pastor implying science was irrelevant because "the world is gonna burn anyway"; a traveling apologist attacking evolution; a B-grade Christian movie that tried to blame science for the evils of the world; material sold in the church bookstore advocating young-earth creationism.

I read many of these books. They promoted the idea that God and science were at war, disparaged those who believed the universe was older than six thousand years, and even suggested that dinosaurs lived harmoniously with Adam and Eve in Eden. In high school, I read a popular one that was big enough to kill a dinosaur. I'll never forget this line:

> One can be a Christian and an evolutionist, just as one can be a Christian thief, or a Christian adulterer, or a Christian liar. It is absolutely impossible for those who profess to believe the Bible to follow Christ and to embrace evolutionism.[3]

Absolutely impossible?

It wasn't like I was specifically told science was evil, but the cumulative effect of that particular brand of Christian subculture was that I had a hard time trusting science. Science was like that awkward relative at Thanksgiving. Someone went rogue and invited them, but nearly everyone was uncomfortable.

A recent study from the Pew Research Center reveals 59 percent of Americans believe there is a conflict between science and religion.[4] There is a widespread cultural assumption that the two are mutually exclusive, thus one must choose between one or the other. According to the philosopher Alvin Plantinga,

> Like it or not . . . there is and has been at any rate apparent conflict. Many Christians have at least the vague impression that modern science is somehow unfriendly to religious belief;

for other believers, it is less a vague impression than a settled conviction.[5]

What's ironic is that Christians aren't the only ones who think science and faith are incompatible. Leading atheist writers and thinkers strongly advocate similar ideas. For example, Jerry Coyne, a professor at the University of Chicago, wrote about this misconception:

> Science and religion, then, are competitors in the business of finding out what is true about our universe. In this goal religion has failed miserably, for its tools for discerning "truth" are useless. These areas are incompatible in precisely the same way, and in the same sense, that rationality is incompatible with irrationality.[6]

Fascinating. So, according to Coyne, not only are religion and science incompatible, but those who believe in religion are *irrational*.

The Jewish mystic Baal Shem Tov once told a story of a deaf man who stepped into the town square. A violinist was playing beautifully, and the villagers were swept up into the moment—dancing, moving, swaying to the melody. The deaf man watched, bewildered. And then he walked away, deciding they were all deluded.[7]

For some atheists, that's how the world works. Believers in God are the mad ones. They can't understand why we dance or why, like Nunez in "The Country of the Blind," we see something they don't. It's not logical or scientific.

So, on one side we have atheists who deride the music of religion, labeling it as an enemy of science. And on the other we have influential Christians deconstructing science, branding it as the enemy of faith.

Where does that leave the rest of us?

Well, that's what's so tragic. In this polarized environment, followers of Jesus feel like they're confined in the middle. We falsely believe we have to choose. It's either the Word or the world. The way of God or the way of man. Faith or science.

We feel torn. Our hearts cling to faith. But our minds can't ignore the science.

Furthermore, when we engage with scientific facts and learn, we see a radical incongruence between what both sides are saying. For example:

- We listen to a lecture and hear the universe isn't six thousand years old but four billion. We see evidence backing up that claim.
- We read an intelligent explanation of what evolution is and isn't. And we wonder how we had so many misconceptions about it.
- On Sunday morning we hear a pastor talk about Jesus turning water into wine. Monday morning, a college professor says miracles are just superstitious legends.

The more we learn, the more our feeling that we can't have it both ways seems confirmed. Either our faith is wrong or science is wrong.

It's in that conflicted space that our doubt grows.

I once read an article in the *Wall Street Journal* in which the comedian Ricky Gervais (who created the British version of *The Office*) published his deconversion story.[8] Like many in the West, he was raised going to church and believing in God. He recalled how, as a child, he experienced a keen sense of wonder when he gazed on the beautiful world that God had made. He was in awe at the resplendant perfection of nature and animals. But then, at the age of eight, his religious framework suddenly collapsed. He heard his older brother talk about atheism. He asked questions, began processing his views on religion, and then turned from his childhood faith. Reflecting on this time, Ricky discussed how his atheism opened the door to a better appreciation and understanding of how the world worked. He felt that belief in God had hindered his development, but once he left faith behind he discovered the richness of a scientific worldview.

In his mind, God and science are irreconcilable. They're at war. God loses. Science wins. End of story.

But that's what's so heartbreaking. The story doesn't have to end that way. And for millions of people who feel they have to choose between science and faith, the story doesn't have to end that way either.

Science and faith are not incompatible.

They are not at war.

They are not enemies.

Let's think about what science is for a second. A quick Google search defines it as "the systematic study of the structure and behavior of the physical and natural world through observation and experiment."

That's it.

Science tells us what the world is like. It pulls things apart. It unmasks the machinery of the natural world. It probes, seeks, investigates, and asks.

Religion gives us another perspective. It tells us what the world means. It puts things back together. It unmasks the Creator of the natural world.

Science only tells us part of the story. It reveals and enriches our perception of reality; opening our eyes to the complexity and splendor of the world. But it cannot tell us why it takes our breath away. According to Rabbi Jonathan Sacks,

> Science analyses, religion integrates. . . . Science tells us what is. Religion tells us what ought to be. Science describes. Religion beckons, summons, calls. Science sees objects. Religion speaks to us as subjects. Science practices detachment. Religion is the art of attachment, self to self, soul to soul. Science sees the underlying order of the physical world. Religion hears the music beneath the noise. Science is the conquest of ignorance. Religion is the redemption of solitude.[9]

Both science and religion explore, investigate, and inquire. Religion, however, goes one step further by looking beyond a narrow, materialistic view of the world. Religion seeks truth in all things. It gently lifts our eyes from the mud to the stars. It dares to whisper the words of Hamlet: "There are more things in heaven and earth, Horatio, than are dreamt of in your philosophy."[10]

Very little of what makes us human can be scientifically understood. And I'm not talking about synapses and cells. I'm talking about weighty human impulses to love, forgive, hope, dream, make moral choices, help those in need, and to live for something more than ourselves. We have a piercing awareness we're more than our physicality. We're haunted by the sense there is a bigger story to be told. If you picked up a book and just read the footnotes, you may get a rudimentary sense of what the book is about, but you would lose the plot. Or, if you ordered an ice cream and decided to only eat the cone, it might taste good, but you're kind of missing the point.

When faith is juxtaposed against science, your view of the world, and yourself, is diminished. But when science and faith converge, your horizon dramatically expands. You pursue more, see more, anticipate more. Your love for God and this world intensifies. In 1 Corinthians 3:21 Paul said: "All things are yours." What this means is that everything in God's creation is an opportunity to discover. Biology, chemistry, physiology, neurology, psychology, and astronomy give us three-dimensional insight into the heart of God. We don't abandon them. We study them, celebrate them; we move them forward.

All things are yours!

If God is the ocean, then science is the vessel that explores the depths of his beauty and creativity. That is why, of all people, followers of Jesus should be leading the charge in the sciences.

But what does that look like? How can we be a voice for both science and faith?

Here's a good place to start: we have to deconstruct the myth that science and faith are at war.

Now, I admit, there have been times, at a superficial level, when it appeared that they were. History is replete with depressing stories of the church questioning or even hindering the advance of science. There are also stories of scientists who opposed Christianity and everything it stood for.

But, as Alvin Plantinga so brilliantly argues in his book, *Where the Conflict Really Lies*, the real conflict isn't between science and religion but naturalism and religion.[11] Naturalism is an atheistic worldview that leaves no room for God, miracles, or the afterlife.

Whenever these ideas are smuggled into the scientific process, then of course it will lead to conflict. But science alone doesn't eliminate religion. In fact, many scientists in history believed just the opposite.

We started the chapter with Francis Bacon, one of the most prominent scientists in history, who was also a passionate theist. But there are so many more. For example, Blaise Pascal, who invented the calculator; Robert Boyle, the founder of modern chemistry; Isaac Newton, who laid the foundation for classical mechanics; Michael Faraday, who is responsible for modern uses of electricity; Charles Babbage, who invented the concept of a programmable computer (essentially the Bill Gates of the 1800s); Gregor Mendel, the founder of the science of genetics; and the infamous astronomer Galileo, who redefined our place in the universe; just to name a few. Galileo once said, "I do not feel obliged to believe that the same God who has endowed us with senses, reason, and intellect has intended us to forgo their use."[12]

And these are just the old, dead guys.

According to the 2009 Pew Forum, 51 percent of scientists today believe in some deity or higher power.[13] These include thinkers like Simon Morris, Alister McGrath, Hugh Ross, Denis Alexander, Monica Grady, Mary Schweitzer, Werner Arber, Katharine Hayhoe, Ben Carson, and Darrel Falk. Francis Collins, the director of the National Institutes of Health, is also a committed Christian. He claims, "The God of the Bible is the God of the genome. God can be found in the cathedral or in the laboratory."[14]

For these scientists (and countless others), belief in God isn't a hindrance to science but is actually the main inspiration for it.

Why is that the case?

Because, as Bacon pointed out, at its core, Christianity insists

God has given us the two books of his Word and his world. And we are invited to uncover what those books have to say. The truth is that when we take a closer look at Scripture, and in particular the words of Jesus, we will find a faith that says, "All questions are welcomed here." Indifference is renounced. Curiosity is welcomed with open arms.

Jesus' first words to his disciples were, "Come and follow me." To say yes to him is to say yes to a life of unending discovery. Christianity is a journey, an adventure, a quest. And this was how Jesus led his disciples forward: by encouraging exploration through inquiry. In fact, questions were his primary mode of facilitating growth in their lives:

- "Do you believe that I am able to do this?" (Matthew 9:28)
- "What do you want me to do for you?" (Luke 18:41)
- "Do you love me?" (John 21:17)
- "Why do you call me, 'Lord, Lord,' and do not do what I say?" (Luke 6:46)
- "Why are you so afraid?" (Matthew 8:26)
- "Who do you say I am?" (Mark 8:29)

More than three hundred times in the Gospels, Jesus peppered his followers with a dazzling array of questions, and as they responded, they had to honestly evaluate and open up their hearts. The questions challenged their presuppositions, equipped them with truth, and led them into a robust, more authentic faith. Jesus also invited them to ask him questions. And they did. More than 180 times, people asked Jesus about life, suffering, relationships, finances, and the kingdom of God. Sometimes Jesus answered directly. But most of the time he responded to their questions with more questions. For example, in Mark 8, when his disciples asked how he was going to feed a hungry crowd, he responded by asking, "How many loaves do you have?" They were expecting a miracle. They thought he'd snap his fingers and a line of food trucks would appear. But Jesus wasn't trying to create passive consumers; he wanted to cultivate passionate disciples. He pushed his followers into the story. And when they took the step, sure enough, they met a lad who had five loaves and two fish. Jesus prayed for the lunch, broke it, and handed it to his disciples, who shared it with the people. Miraculously, everyone had more than enough.

Jesus stretched his disciples way beyond their comfort zones. And then some. He confronted them, urged them forward, and led them into difficult situations. He was anything but passive. He jolted them out of the comforts of conformity. He relished the banter. He asked questions. Lots and lots of questions.

Why? Because questions strip away our defenses. They open our eyes to dimensions we may have never considered.

In 1944, Isidor Isaac Rabi became a Nobel laureate for his discovery of nuclear magnetic resonance. He once attributed his success as a scientist to the way his mother greeted him after school. Most mothers would ask their children, "Did you learn anything today?" But Rabi's mother asked him, "Did you ask a good question today?"[15]

Like Rabi's mother, Jesus cultivated a similar ethos of openness and curiosity. And for hundreds of years, Christians understood this. They recognized that a static faith is a contradiction, but a vibrant faith pushes fiercely into the unknown. Is it any wonder, then, why some of history's leading scientists were also followers of Jesus?

It shouldn't surprise us.

The British scholar James Hannam, in his book *God's*

Philosophers: How the Medieval World Laid the Foundations of Modern Science, said, "Christian theology turned out to be uniquely suited to encouraging the study of the natural world, because this was believed to be God's creation."[16] Christians celebrated and advocated science, because it was an inescapable byproduct of their devotion to God. God was the creator, and they were the curators. They saw beauty in nature, and were motivated to understand it, because they believed in a beautiful God.

Deep in our spiritual DNA is a relentless desire to understand how the world works. We long to open the hood and get our hands dirty. It's only natural. And we come from a long line of people who did just that. They celebrated science, championed its discoveries, enabled its progress, gazed on its endless symmetry and artistry, and then passionately worshipped the Artist.

Now that is a story worth telling.

And what a different story that is from the myopic, polarizing one we're told today. The idea that science and faith are incompatible is so boring, lifeless, and flat. Nothing could be further from the truth.

» «

But, if science and faith are not at war, what about those times when science tells us things that seem to contradict what we think Scripture says? For example:

- Recent discoveries imply Adam and Eve may have never existed.
- The Big Bang theory and modern cosmology versus "let there be light."

- Evolution versus instantaneous creation.
- Questionable evidence for a global flood in Noah's time.
- Archaeological findings that seem to rewrite stories in the Bible.
- The incompatibility of modern understandings of the human body versus biblical accounts of supernatural healing.

Each of these issues opens a huge can of worms, and there's no way to adequately sift through them all in a single chapter. So, in celebration of liberated worms, let me allow them to roam freely and instead offer a few thoughts.

As Christians, our starting point is Genesis 1:1: "In the beginning God created . . ." Once we believe that, then the most important question of our lives has been answered. Everything else flows from it. He's the Creator. How he did it is secondary. That's where science comes in.

Of course, there will be times when there is a perceived conflict between our understanding of Scripture and science. We're human and fallible. So is science. Science doesn't always get it right. Astronomers were once convinced the earth was the center of the universe (and so was the church, for that matter). Then Copernicus, who was a committed Christian, discovered we weren't the center of everything. And so, we invented selfies to make ourselves feel better.

It's not just our interpretation of science that is fallible. So is our interpretation of Scripture. Knowingly or unknowingly, we can manipulate the Bible, trying to make it say what we want it to say. Augustine warned us about this in the fifth century. In one of his commentaries on Genesis, he cautioned against trying to squeeze science into our theological boxes, calling it "a disgraceful and dangerous thing."[17] Instead, he argued, we should consider what we know is true about nature, then come back to Scripture with humility. Maybe we've been reading it all wrong. Maybe there's hyperbole we've missed, or subtlety, nuance, sarcasm, humor. Maybe some parts are poetry, not history. Maybe we've been reading it too literally.

When Jesus said he is the door, he was not saying he's made out of wood. Something else is going on. We need to look beyond what we assume the Bible is saying and invest time to grasp its original intent and context. As we do, we'll not only learn more about what the Bible meant but who we are meant to be. We'll see it with fresh eyes.

We also need to be careful that we don't try to squeeze God into the gaps of what we don't understand scientifically. I recently saw a YouTube debate in which a Christian was asserting that scientific mysteries are proof for the existence of God. Now, there's a lot we don't know about biology, gravity, quantum mechanics, superstring theory, and the nature of light, but these riddles in and of themselves do not solve the question of God's existence. Scientific mysteries may point us to him, give us clues that he is there, even provide archetypes for theological reflection, but they're not the basis for our faith. Ignorance is a poor apologetic.

Christians can easily fall into this trap (atheists can too, but in a different way). The problem, however, is that it can lead to a crisis of faith when certain mysteries are resolved. It also makes us susceptible to arguments like this: "We now have telescopes, microscopes, computers, smartphones, and antibiotics. We don't need God anymore. People used to believe in him when they didn't know how the world worked, but now science has made God irrelevant."

When we hear this false narrative, our faith can be shaken. We doubt. We may even assume that science is the enemy of faith.

But this is an incredibly shortsighted way of looking at it, especially when the truth is so much bigger.

God is not the God of the gaps. He is the God of everything. What we know and what we don't. It is all his design. Write down everything you know about science and include a question mark for everything you don't. Then draw a massive circle around it all. That's God. The universe is complicated and full of mystery because he made it that way. And then he gave it to us.

All things are yours.

God is within, around, above, below, and beyond science. A scientific discovery doesn't negate the existence of God any more than understanding how an iPhone works negates the existence of Tim Cook. John Lennox writes,

> It is likewise a category mistake to suppose that our understanding of the impersonal principles according to which the universe works makes it either unnecessary or impossible to believe in the existence of a personal Creator . . . we should not confuse the mechanisms by which the universe works either with its cause or its upholder.[18]

This is *so* important. Science doesn't explain away God. It just shows us how creative and beautiful he is.

But what if there seems to be a clear conflict between God's Word and God's world?

Look closer. Investigate more. Probe. Inquire. Wait. Study. Read. Ask questions. Be open to the idea that your analysis of Scripture (or science) is wrong. Don't abandon your faith. Don't give up what you love most for what you know least. Embrace the wonder of unknowing. Sit in the tension. Be okay with mystery.

And here's the good news: as followers of Jesus we believe that someday every mystery will be resolved. Creation will encounter its Creator. Science and faith will coalesce, mind and spirit will unite, and all will fade into worship. In that moment, as we step into eternity, we'll discover there wasn't a conflict after all.

Chapter 7

Why Is the World So Broken?

*Lament is the voice of that pain . . . for the mountain
of suffering of humanity and creation itself.
Lament is the voice of faith struggling to live with
unanswered questions and unexplained suffering.*
—CHRISTOPHER WRIGHT

*My wound is an unanswered question. The wounds
of all humanity are unanswered questions.*
—NICHOLAS WOLTERSTORFF

WE SAT TOGETHER IN a circle as a group of women from ages ten to twenty-two began to share their stories. I was in Kampala, Uganda, along with a small group of pastors from Portland, to visit and encourage ministries that our church supports. One of these ministries is a safe house for women who need refuge and healing from sexual brokenness. In partnership with Bob Goff and his organization Love Does, we built the house to provide protection, education, counseling, and hope.

We listened as they shared. Their stories were devastating.

One young woman stood up. Slowly, in a gentle whisper, she began to describe her tragic past. She grew up in poverty. She spent years living on the streets, doing her best to survive. She was forced into prostitution. She was raped by a family member. And then, tragically, one of her parents died.

When she reached that part of the story, she paused, looking around the room. Her eyes looked hollow, like an empty well. And then, from some unspoken place inside her, the dam burst.

She began sobbing. And so did we. The other women immediately gathered around her, praying for her, speaking kind words over her, affirming her, loving her. She looked up and told us all how thankful she was for the home, her new friends, and a God who loved her so much. It was a moment both heartbreaking and yet full of unspeakable hope.

A few days later we drove north to the city of Gulu, in northern Uganda. Gulu has a tragic past and is still reeling from the devastation and chaos of war. Signs of trauma are everywhere. Beginning in the late 1980s through 2006, a violent, cult-like militia called the LRA, led by Joseph Kony, sprang up and ravaged the city. Homes were obliterated, people were murdered, 1.9 million were displaced from their homes, and thirty thousand children were kidnapped.

Thirty thousand.

The number is staggering. These are young, innocent lives violently robbed of childhood and forced to become soldiers.

In recent years, Kony's army has been decimated and is no longer as severe a threat. Some say he is hiding somewhere in the jungles of the Congo. Most of his soldiers are either dead or have returned home.

The challenges for these former child soldiers are indescribable. Some of the boys, when they were first abducted, were forced to kill members of their own families. Some of the girls, now young women, have returned home with babies. They've known nothing but violence and bloodshed. And now, back in Gulu, they're trying to adjust to "normal" life.

But how could life ever be normal after that? How do you heal? How do you come to terms with your own pain? We met some of these former child soldiers and heard their stories. Words cannot express how tragic they were.

On our second night in the city, I was introduced to the most remarkable woman I've ever met in my life: Sister Rosemary. In 2014 she was called one of *Time* magazine's 100 Most Influential People in the World. In 2017 she was nominated for the Nobel Peace Prize. Her life is one of boundless sacrifice, forgiveness, hope, and courage. While Joseph Kony was terrorizing the region, she bravely and quietly fought back. She opened her convent for thousands of children who were seeking refuge. She refused to leave even when her own life was in danger. She loved the city, serving it selflessly through its darkest days. She then started an all-girls school for former child soldiers. These women, shattered by the desolation of war, are now loved, mentored, and equipped with practical skills to help them readapt to life in the community.

Sister Rosemary radiates joy. It's like it can't be contained. It sparkles, flashes, builds up, and explodes out of her. She smiles and laughs constantly, and it's unbelievably contagious. We sat down for a simple meal of rice and chicken, and within moments I was laughing too.

And then it hit me. How could a woman who has personally experienced so much and witnessed unimaginable depths of suffering exude such authentic joy? How did she reconcile her faith with the brokenness of her city?

I had to ask her.

She, still smiling and with eyes beaming, began to answer.

I'll never forget what she had to say.

» «

Before we get to Sister Rosemary's words, we need to first acknowledge that of all the issues that haunt our faith, the question of suffering is, by far, the most disturbing.

Why did God allow the young women I met in Kampala to be abused? Why does he allow entire cities to be devastated by war? Why does he allow violence, tragedy, genocide, and ethnic cleansing? Why are there natural disasters that randomly destroy communities? Why leukemia, cancer, and heart disease? Why starvation, racism, sexism, and oppression of the weak? Why doesn't God stop human trafficking? Why is there so much injustice and inequality?

We live in the shrapnel of a broken world. Suffering threatens us, assails us, and violates us. And then it defies us to try and make sense of it all. How could this happen? What is the point? How do we resolve what we know about God with so many stories of grief?

The world weeps. And so do we.

And, it is there, in the midst of our tears, that we begin to question our faith. We ask why. We doubt. We shake our fist. We may even question the existence of God. Or, at the very least, his willingness to help. Suffering shatters the illusion of certainty. It breaks open the hidden parts of us, leaving us vulnerable and exposed. In the presence of unanswered, or unanswerable, questions, we stand alone. God, meanwhile, seems absent.

>> <<

Where is God when we need him most?

Rabbi Jonathan Sacks concludes,

This question . . . causes more people to lose faith than any other. There is none deeper. To fail to take it seriously is to fail to be serious at all. It is the question of questions, and it calls for nothing less than total honesty.[1]

And so, let's be honest.

If God is all powerful and all loving, then why does evil exist? Why does the world bleed with suffering? Why doesn't he intervene?

To be human is to grapple with that question, and for thousands of years we haven't stopped asking it.

What makes suffering so intensely disorienting is that it not only erodes our confidence in the character of God, it also devastates so much of what gives life meaning. Suffering robs us of things we hold close. It strips us of our humanity. We're left reeling; torn between the apparent pointlessness of a broken world and the impulse to comprehend it.

In philosophy, efforts to intellectually explain suffering is called a theodicy. And every ideology, including atheism, attempts to do so. Hinduism tries to explain suffering as Karma, the belief that tragedy is a byproduct of our own failures. If you're in pain, it's because you did something wrong, either in this life or the last. When I was in India, I saw the devastating effects of this: people relegated to caste systems, discriminated against, trapped in an endless cycle of poverty because they saw no way out.

Buddhism also explains suffering as the result of Karma. It teaches that if we can obtain enlightenment and a "calmness in the soul," we will see suffering is an illusion, and we will be liberated. In Islam, suffering is a result of unbelief; God is absolved of responsibility because of human wickedness. In Animism, suffering can be due to a moral failure or not doing enough to appease the gods. New Age teaches that suffering is part of the evolutionary process of higher consciousness. Atheism posits that suffering exists because that's how the universe works; we live, we die, and that's it. There's no hope beyond the grave.

Any worldview, to be credible, needs to not only explain but inspire. But to do that, it has to grapple with the question of suffering in a clear and compelling way.

It is the most important question of all. And of all the questions I've grappled with on my journey of faith and doubt, it is the hardest to understand.

So how does the Bible engage with this question? What answers does Christianity provide? What can it say to the child soldier, the victim of rape, the widow, the orphan, the homeless, and the single mom? The Jewish Holocaust scholar Irving Greenberg cautioned, "No statement, theological or otherwise, should be made that would not be credible in the presence of burning children."[2]

Wow.

That is why I'm so reluctant to make this chapter a checklist of philosophical and theological answers, because it doesn't actually help when you're being torn apart by grief. There's nothing worse than trying to make sense of heartache only to have someone say, "Well, I'm sure God is teaching you all kinds of things through this." Or, "It's okay. God is on the throne." Or, even worse, "You may have lost someone, but God gained another angel."

That doesn't help.

Now, this doesn't mean there aren't all kinds of interesting answers out there. For millennia, thinkers, theologians, rabbis, scholars, and philosophers have agonized over this issue. Some suggest that the reason there is so much suffering in the world is because of human free will. We chose to walk away from God in Eden, and we keep making that choice every day. Therefore, the evil that we see around us is just a reflection of the evil that lives within.

Other theologians, like the early church leader Irenaeus, suggested that God allows suffering in order to dignify and refine our character. Romans 5:3–4 says, "We also glory in our sufferings, because we know that suffering produces perseverance; perseverance, character; and character, hope." Suffering, then, has redemptive power.

Kierkegaard spoke of this in terms of art. He asked, "What is a poet? An unhappy man who hides deep anguish in his heart, but whose lips are so formed that when the sigh and cry pass through them, it sounds like lovely music."[3] There are times when the only way character is composed is through the song of suffering. It expands our love. It weaves grace into our heart, and places us in solidarity with the wounded of the world. It shatters the mirage of self-reliance and moves us past the superficial.

Another well-known theodicy blames suffering on cosmic evil, satanic powers, and demons. This is sometimes called a "warfare theodicy." In this view, God and Satan are at war, and we are caught in the crossfire. Clark Pinnock wrote, "Jesus did not attribute things like deformity, blindness, leprosy and fever to the providence of God. He regarded them as evidence of the reign of darkness."[4] So if a family is killed in a fire, a famine ravages South Sudan, or a cluster bomb is dropped on a village in war, it's a microcosm of a much larger war between the kingdom of God and Satan. The earth is a battlefield, and the only recourse is to confront and overcome the enemy's attack.

Each of these theodicies can be incredibly helpful in their own way. They provide compelling and biblical answers and help us understand why we suffer. The problem is, they can only go so far. Or, they don't go far enough. They're insufficient. And, if I'm brutally honest, they don't always work.

For example, blaming suffering on human free will doesn't resolve the tragedy of birth defects or natural disasters. Likewise, saying that suffering is a tool for growth and character development doesn't account for gratuitous, debilitating circumstances that cause irreparable harm. Some things are so tragic that they leave us scarred for life. What doesn't kill us doesn't always make us stronger. And while Satan *is* the ultimate enemy, stalking our planet and unleashing misery upon it, this doesn't explain why God allows him to do it in the first place. Why doesn't he just annihilate him right now?

In and of themselves, theodicies are not enough. They help, they can be a wonderful place to start, and they may even lead us to a place where healing can begin. But they aren't able to fully resolve our deepest doubts. Trying to explain suffering with theodicies can feel like trying to kill a giant with a bag of small stones. David did it, but for most of us, we're still faced with the question, *Why?*

The truth is, suffering will persist until the Man of Sorrows overcomes it. Until then, we won't understand it fully. "We see through a glass darkly" (1 Cor. 13:12 KJV).

Maybe that's why, before trying to neatly resolve the problem of suffering, the Bible first introduces us to the One who walks with us through it. A God that loves, pursues, and, more than that, suffers alongside us in our times of doubt.

Millenia ago, Babylonian myths such as the Enuma Elish taught that the world was created out of a violent struggle between the gods. Emerging from the chaos, humankind. But even then, we were an afterthought. The gods had their own dramas to settle; we were just irrelevant, distant bystanders.

But the book of Genesis describes a God who is *near*. A God who cares. A God who created not out of war but love. From humanity's first breath, this God was tirelessly invested. He walked with Adam in the cool of the day. He spoke to him, cared for him, and invited him to enjoy his beautiful creation.

Suffering, evil, war, disease, cancer, unemployment, anxiety, depression, and loneliness—this was not God's plan for the world. And even when humanity turned its back on God, he refused to stop loving them. He sought them when they were hiding, covered their nakedness, and gave them the unconditional promise of redemption.

But didn't God kick them out of the garden of Eden? Yes, because sin isolates, divides, and destroys. Sin is the alienation of the soul from God. But what I love about the God of the Bible is that he left the garden too.

He pursued his creation. He refused to leave their side.

He was with them in the desert, while they wandered homeless for forty years. He was with them when they were surrounded by enemies and trembling with fear. He comforted them as they sought him on the mountain, wept in the temple, and cried out to him when they were in exile. He was unrelenting, unyielding, ever present, and ever faithful. He gave them this promise:

> Do not fear, for I have redeemed you;
> I have summoned you by name; you are mine.
> When you pass through the waters, I will be with you;
> And when you pass through the rivers, they will not sweep
>   over you.
> When you walk through the fire, you will not be burned;
> The flames will not set you ablaze. (Isaiah 43:1–2)

Earlier in the same book, God spoke of a day when a virgin would give birth to a son called Immanuel, which means "God with us" (Isaiah 7:14). Eight hundred years after this promise, Jesus was born. God's answer to suffering isn't found in complex theodicies, clever philosophical arguments, or religious clichés; it's found in his Son.

In Jesus, we meet a God who suffers. We meet a God who doesn't just acknowledge our pain but enters into it. Jesus initiated the defeat of suffering by suffering himself. He was born in poverty, experienced racism, was rejected by his friends, and then was betrayed with a kiss. He was beaten, mocked, spat upon, and nailed to a cross.

This is no deistic God, aloof and uncaring, but one who smashes the door down and shares our brokenness.

For us to begin to comprehend the absurdity of evil, we have to start with the God who is near.

» «

In John 11, Jesus experienced the death of a close friend, and he wept. The omniscient, omnipresent, omnipotent God of the universe wept. The tears of God mingled with the tears of the world.

Sometimes the only appropriate response to suffering is boundless grief. The ancient Hebrews used the word *lament*.

Lament is the cry of a heart that is shattered, raw, and largely unhealed. It gazes into suffering, is bruised by its ragged edges, staggers, weeps, and cries out for justice. Lament resists shallow, packaged, simplistic answers. It demands fierce authenticity and is unafraid of unanswerable questions.

Lament is the song of the doubting soul.

We live in an age, however, when lament has fallen on hard times. We don't know how to handle grief. We prefer denial. We are the most medicated nation ever. Images and stories of suffering unsettle us. We're numbed by entertainment and digitized distractions. We're intoxicated by comfort. And then, when anguish opens up violent questions about God and life, we repress and conceal it. But that can only work for so long. Grief is like a river cresting its banks; we can deny or strive to contain the impending flood or learn how to live in deeper water.

Scripture is dripping with the stories of men and women who did just that. They saw what was happening around them, named the injustice, and cried out for God to explain himself. David screamed, "How long, LORD?" (Psalm 13:1). Jeremiah, overwhelmed by the oppression he witnessed, implored God to intervene. Job despaired. Jacob wrestled. Moses challenged. Abraham doubted. Mary questioned. Jesus wept.

Lament is not the antithesis of faith; it is what faith looks like when it draws near to grief. The more passionately we believe in the goodness of God, the more passionately we protest when his goodness is obscured.

That is why Jesus wept at his friend's tomb.

It's okay to give voice to our loneliness. It's okay to shout our dissent. It's okay to be angry.

It's okay not to have all the answers.

God still runs to us, embraces us, and weeps with us there.

And then, through our tears, we notice that the weeping one has scarred hands. His body is broken. His faced disfigured.

We realize he has suffered too.

Second Corinthians 5:21 says, "God made him who had no sin to be sin for us, so that in him we might become the righteousness of God." At the cross, Jesus became what he was not so that we might become who he has called us to be. You know the value of something based on how much someone pays for it. The cross means that you are unimaginably loved by God. His suffering was our redemption. His death our hope. Henri Blocher reminds us, "We have no other position than at the foot of the cross . . . God's answer is evil turned back upon itself, conquered by the ultimate degree of love in the fulfillment of justice."[5]

When Jesus died on the cross, which was a barbaric Roman invention explicitly designed for torture, he took the ultimate crime—killing God—and redeemed it. Nietzsche may have written, "God is dead," but that's only part of the story. Three days later the crucified One rose again, shattering the chains of death. The cross, once the embodiment and manifestation of everything evil, is now our triumph, hope, and salvation.

I like to call this "judo theology." I remember taking judo lessons as a kid. The whole idea is to use the power of an opponent against themselves. If someone throws a punch, you maneuver yourself in such a way that their own attack brings them down. In many ways, that's what happened when Jesus died. Satan threw at Jesus everything he had—hatred, anguish, loneliness, relentless pain and suffering—and Jesus bore it, endured it, and ultimately redeemed it.

Jesus overcame evil with good.

And that's what we're called to do as well.

We may not understand suffering, but we can fight against it. We may not know why the world is so broken, but we can try to put it back together. We can resist. We can defend what remains. We can be a voice of healing. We can advance the way of love. We can pray. In the face of injustice, prayer is a revolution of hope.

When Jesus prayed, "Your kingdom come, your will be done, on earth as it is in heaven" (Matthew 6:10), what he meant is that we are invited to join God in his mission to restore and renew all things. We get to be his hands and feet in the world. The sixteenth-century mystic Teresa of Avila said,

> Christ has no body now but yours.
> No hands, no feet on earth but yours.
> Yours are the eyes through which he looks compassion on this
>   world.
> Yours are the feet with which he walks to do good.
> Yours are the hands with which he blesses all the world.[6]

We are what redemption looks like. This means that, because of grace, everything in your story has purpose. Even the dark parts. Especially the dark parts. Your brokenness is what allows the light to get in.

It's judo theology. We overcome evil with good.

And someday, evil will be overcome.

The last book of the Bible speaks of a day when God will wipe away every tear from our eyes. There will be no more death or mourning or crying or pain (Revelation 21:4). A day of restoration is coming and, from the ashes of our fallen world, a new one will emerge. Death will be defeated. Suffering will be destroyed. Everything that is broken will be made new.

If you don't believe in God, these are just empty words. In atheism, there is no room for justice, healing, or hope. If God does not exist, then our tears mean nothing. Our shouts reverberate into the void. Even protest is futile, because there is no one who hears our cries.

But if God does exist, then what Jesus did when he died and rose again is just a foretaste of what he will do with all creation. Creation groans, it suffers, it aches for the day of redemption, but someday it will resurrect into new life. In the words of Tolkien, everything sad will "come untrue."

A few years ago I had a chance to visit the Vatican in Rome. I was mesmerized by the Sistine Chapel, Michelangelo's creative genius, and the brilliance of Raphael's *Transfiguration*. So much to see and take in. At one point, I paused to look at Renaissance-era tapestries in the Vatican museum. On one side, there were intricate displays of stories, battles, people, and places, all masterfully woven together with tiny pieces of string! But what's interesting is that if you look at the back of the tapestry, it's a cacophony of wild, jumbled, tangled, knotted threads. No order. No design. It's haphazard and confusing.

On one side is chaos. On the other side, beauty.[7]

What if heaven is simply the movement from one side of the tapestry to the other? What if redemption is God taking everything that's wild, jumbled, and chaotic in our lives and weaving something beautiful out of it? At present, our perspective, like a heavy veil, obscures what that could look like. But someday we will move past the veil and see face-to-face. Paul wrote in 2 Corinthians 4:17–18:

> For our light and momentary troubles are achieving for us an eternal glory that far outweighs them all. So we fix our eyes not on what is seen, but on what is unseen, since what is seen is temporary, but what is unseen is eternal.

On that day, when faith becomes sight, we will see what is now unseen. Our doubts will collapse. We will see him. The Lamb that was slain. The crucified God. The Man of Sorrows.

And we will enter his rest.

» «

For me, the only way to make any sense of suffering is through the lens of eternity. I love how Dostoyevsky put it:

> I believe like a child that suffering will be healed and made up for, that all the humiliating absurdity of human contradictions will vanish like a pitiful mirage . . . that in the world's finale, at the moment of eternal harmony, something so precious will come to pass that it will suffice for all hearts, for the comforting of all resentments, for the atonement of all the crimes of humanity . . . that it will make it not only possible to forgive— but to justify all that has happened . . . [8]

"Suffering will be healed and made up for."
I have no idea how that will happen. My perspective is too

limited. My ideas of an eternal heaven are warped and twisted by my smallness; my thoughts of God's power are held back by my weakness.

But I do believe God is able. I believe in the God of hope. I believe God can do more than I could ever ask, think, or imagine.

Until that day, we do our best to tie the broken threads of our world back together. We weep, we doubt, we protest, we lament the presence of evil. We do everything in our power to overcome it with good. We cry out for God's kingdom to come and his will to be done on earth as it is in heaven. And then we link arms with God to help make that hope a reality.

» «

Which brings me back to Sister Rosemary.

As I sat with her in Gulu, bearing all the questions and weight of the stories I had heard, she set down her fork and told me that, while she didn't know why there was so much suffering in the world, she still believed in a God who could restore what evil and sin had torn apart.

She told me that love is greater than hate.

She told me that forgiveness is stronger than bitterness.

She told me that kindness can heal even the most devastated heart.

She then said, "I've seen what hope can do. And I've devoted the rest of my life to being that hope for as many people as I can."

And, with a smile, she picked up her fork and resumed eating her chicken and rice.

Chapter 8

Why Is God Silent?

I know that He exists.
Somewhere—in Silence.
—Emily Dickinson

Will you forget me forever? How long
will you hide your face from me?
—Psalm 13:1

THE JOURNEY OF FAITH is most exhilarating when we hear the voice of God. This can happen in a variety of ways. A message at church moves you, a time of worship grips your heart, you witness a healing or miracle, a verse from Scripture lurches off the pages into your life, a door that you thought was bolted shut unexpectedly opens, a prayer is overwhelmingly answered.

Have you ever had an experience like that?

Have you ever had an encounter with God that was so incandescent, vivid, and real, that all you could do is worship? Have you ever heard him speak so clearly and beautifully that it left you speechless?

Times like this can make you feel like you're on the liquid edge between heaven and earth. Your senses quicken. God is closer than your next breath. You're certain you'll never doubt again.

I've had several moments like that in my life.

By far, the most unforgettable was when I returned from Vanuatu and met my future wife, Elyssa.

I was twenty-three years old and had only been back from the jungle for a few days. And I looked like it. My hair was long and wild, my jeans torn and pleading to be thrown away, a worn-out pair of smelly sandals hung off my feet, and, because I hadn't adjusted to the cold Oregon weather, a friend of mine gave me his sweatshirt to wear. I've never seen anything like this sweatshirt. It was so exorbitantly thick that I had a hard time keeping my arms down; it kept wanting me to be a penguin. On the front was an offensively deep, seventies-style V-neck, replete with long, vulgar, wispy strands of white fur protruding violently in all directions. It was a stylistic nightmare. I looked like marshmallow-man-meets-Puff Daddy. Portland hipsters would be mortified.

And it was in that state, standing awkwardly in the lobby of a church, that I met the love of my life.

We shook hands, and she introduced herself. Nervously, I mumbled something back. After three years in the jungle it was probably something like, "Me Dominic, you woman." She was mesmerizing. Her eyes were soft and beautiful. Her voice sweet and sincere. We talked for a couple of hours. I don't remember a word that I said, but it didn't matter. I was captivated.

For several days after that, I couldn't stop thinking about her. I wondered if I would see her again. I kicked myself for not asking for her number.

That same week I was driving in downtown Medford. It was

early, and I was looking for some coffee. As I drove, I prayed: "God, would you just take her out of my mind? I don't want to be distracted right now. I don't want to get involved in something that's not your will." That sounded nice and spiritual. But then I continued, more honestly: "But, God, she sure was amazing, and I'd love to see her again. So, I pray, if it's your will, and if she's the one, may I run into her today. In Jesus' name, amen."

I actually prayed that. I know it sounds ridiculous, but I was in love.

Literally seconds after my earnest prayer, I saw a Starbucks. I pulled into the parking lot and, still wearing my Puff-Daddy sweatshirt, got out of the car. True story, the instant I opened the Starbucks door, I saw her standing in front of me just two feet away!

As if she had been waiting for me her entire life.

The angels of God filled the room with a rousing Hallelujah chorus.

I laughed. "What are you doing here?"

She smiled. "Well, I work here and just got on my break."

I couldn't believe it. Talk about an answered prayer! We sat down for coffee, and the rest is history.

>> <<

Moments like this, when God makes his will so unmistakably clear, are among the most beautiful experiences in life. Hearing him, seeing him work, sensing his presence—it's like air in our lungs. Our souls come alive. It's as if time freezes and all of life suddenly snaps into focus. We long for this.

My brother-in-law works on tall ships. You know, the kind you see in pirate movies or ancient ports. One of the things I've learned about the history of shipbuilding and navigation is that when a ship needed to recalibrate its compass, the captain would dispatch someone carrying the compass to the top of a mast. The reason he did that was because the compass had to rise above the influence of the iron hull. Once taken higher, the compass would readjust and point to true north.

Likewise, the limits of our vision are determined by the proximity of our love. The higher we climb, the farther we see. Our life resets; in-sync and recalibrated by the sound of God's voice.

Jesus said, "My sheep hear My voice" (John 10:27 NKJV). And when we do, it's wonderful. The influence of the superficial recedes, and we see with piercing clarity the way to go.

But what about those times when we can't hear him? What about those prayers that go unanswered? What if we climb the mast only to find there's nothing there?

» «

One of the most thought-provoking books I've ever read is the masterpiece *Silence* by Shusaku Endo. In it, he recounts the heartbreaking story of Jesuit priest and missionary Father Sebastien Rodrigues. He moved to Japan to learn the truth about his former teacher, Christovao Ferreira, who had supposedly given up his faith. The story is slow, raw, and gut-wrenching. It graphically describes the persecution that Japanese Christians endured during the 1600s.

Rodrigues watched in horror as close friends and members of his church were systematically and cruelly killed. Some were drowned in the ocean; others were left on stakes to die of exhaustion. Rodrigues was spiritually and emotionally devastated by what he saw. Doubt threatened to overwhelm him. He couldn't understand why God allowed innocent people to endure so much misery.

But what traumatized his faith the most was the deafening silence of God:

> What do I want to say? I myself do not quite understand. . . .
> Behind the depressing silence of this sea, the silence of God . . .
> the feeling that while men raise their voices in anguish God remains with folded arms, silent.[1]

The silence of God gradually wore Rodrigues down. Wounded, confused, and disoriented, he asked himself if he believed anything at all. He eventually found his old mentor and discovered the rumors were true: he had apostatized. In horrific circumstances, Rodrigues was then forced to decide if he would as well.

I'll leave it for you to read the story yourself. It's beautiful, disturbing, and relentlessly contends with this question: *Why is God silent?*

Of all the causes of doubt in our lives, this is one of the hardest to fathom.

In some ways it's similar to the doubts we experience when we suffer, but it comes at us in a different way. Suffering-induced doubt is often due to a sudden, catastrophic event, like an earthquake that leaves us ruined. But the silence of God is glacial. It gnaws, corrodes, and sinks into and through us. The philosopher Michael Rea observes,

> God's silence is *painful* for us. Many believers experience crippling doubt, overwhelming sadness, and ultimate loss of

faith as a result of ongoing silence . . . many people have been positively damaged by divine silence.[2]

A silent God sometimes feels like no God, and that can wreak havoc on our faith. And then, like any relationship that's broken, our heart gives way to doubt. We begin to wonder:

- If he promised that he would never leave me or forsake me, why am I so lonely?
- I read the Bible and see stories of God speaking to his people. Why doesn't he do that for me?
- When I pray, it's like my words fall on deaf ears. *Where are you, God?*
- Is God disappointed with me? Have I done something wrong? Why is he holding back?

Have you ever had someone give you the silent treatment? It hurts. When you feel God does the same, it hurts even more.

In Psalm 28:1, David used poetry to describe what this feels like:

> To you, LORD, I call;
> You are my Rock,
> Do not turn a deaf ear to me.
> For if you remain silent,
> I will be like those who go down to the pit.

The word *pit* (רוֹב in Hebrew) can be translated "dungeon." To David, God's silence was a spiritual death sentence, a form of cosmic torture. It broke him. His heart cried out:

You, God, are my God . . .
I thirst for you,
My whole being longs for you,
In a dry and parched land
Where there is no water. (Psalm 63:1)

Notice that David compared the silence of God to thirst. When someone experiences severe physical thirst, it's a medical emergency. Left unchecked it can lead to neurological changes like headaches, confusion, tiredness, and even seizures. Because the body is more than 60 percent water, the cells in your body literally begin to shrink. It's incredibly painful.

When David insisted that he was *thirsty for God*, it was so much more than nice-sounding words to put on a Christian mug. He was describing a spiritual emergency. David was screaming for help.

I'm so thankful that psalms like this are in the Bible, and that God doesn't censor doubt-filled words. If the Bible were nothing more than happy, clappy affirmations of faith, describing how close and tangible God is, it would be hard to relate to. But when David begged God not to be silent, or when he described his spiritual loneliness as thirst, well, that's something I can understand.

Because I've been there too. Many times.

And chances are, you've been there as well.

And it's in that "dry and parched land," when it feels like our soul is estranged from his presence, that we have a decision to make.

Some use the silence of God as a justification for unbelief. I think of the atheist Bertrand Russell who complained that God had given him insufficient evidence to believe and that, if God existed, he ought to do far more to affirm his existence.

Others may not reject God as much as grow indifferent toward him. Perhaps they distance themselves from the community of faith or give up reading Scripture and prayer: "If God doesn't answer me, then I won't ask." Spirituality begins to feel like a dysfunctional, one-way relationship or a breakup, so, to protect their hearts, they put up walls. They insulate, distract, intoxicate, or isolate themselves, whatever numbs them most, as they slowly walk away.

But for others, like David, the silence of God doesn't drive them from faith. Instead, it becomes a catalyst for deeper faith. They turn their desert into a cathedral, weeping, crying, praying, waiting. They pursue the God they can't see. They expect him to speak.

And sometimes he does.

Sometimes he doesn't.

Either way, God's silence creates space for doubt. And either way, we're left with the nagging question: Why doesn't God just clear up the confusion and make his presence known?

This question is surprisingly difficult to answer. Words, no matter how many we use, are insufficient to explain silence. It's like trying to use a flashlight to gaze into a black hole. It devours the very thing you're using to understand it.

But let me begin here.

If you are in a season of silence, you are not alone. Our faith is crammed with the stories of passionate believers in God who went through times like this. We already heard David's rapacious words in the Psalms. But there are so many more:

- The prophet Habakkuk, when he saw his city ruined, cried out, "How long shall I cry, and You will not hear?" (Habakkuk 1:2 NKJV).

- Mother Teresa agonized over the silence of God that left so many "unanswered questions" within her.
- St. John of the Cross, a sixteenth-century Carmelite monk, after being abducted, beaten, and locked away in a window-less cell, wrote, "Where have you hidden, Beloved, and left me moaning? You fled like the stag after wounding me; I went out calling you, but you were gone."[3]
- Job lost everything: his children, possessions, and health. But the salt in the wound was the overwhelming sense that God had abandoned him: "I cry out to you, God, but you do not answer; I stand up, but you merely look at me" (Job 30:20).
- Even Jesus felt abandoned by his Father. When he was suffering on the cross, he asked, "My God, my God, why have you forsaken me?" (Matthew 27:46).

I don't know why the Father was silent when Jesus was on the cross. I don't know why God was silent with Job, Habakkuk, or so many others. But it does lead us to the uncomfortable truth: God's silence is both an esoteric mystery and an unbending reality. If Jesus, who was God, experienced the unbearable silence of God, chances are we will too. It is a normal though baffling part of the journey of faith.

There are times when you're doing all the right things—praying, seeking, worshipping, following God as best as you know how—but still God is silent. And until we can ask him why in heaven, we won't know the reason.

This is why trust is vital.

Like any friendship, sometimes there are periods of silence between you and the other person. When that happens, you can either panic, expect the worst, invent false narratives in your head, doubt their character, or you can trust that they are who you believe them to be.

In Matthew 15 there is a story of a Canaanite woman who was desperate for God to speak: "Lord, Son of David, have mercy on me! My daughter is demon-possessed and suffering terribly" (v. 22). If ever there was a time for Jesus to say something, to generously share encouraging and comforting words, it was then. But the very next verse says he "did not answer." It's hard to read that story and not be frustrated or confused. Why didn't he respond? Why didn't he let her know he cared? If you keep reading, the story gets even more tense, because she wouldn't take silence for an answer. She screamed. She shouted. She pursued him down the busy road. Jesus' disciples begged him to "send her away" (v. 23). She screamed louder.

Then Jesus stopped.

She threw herself before him, sobbing, pleading. He looked at her, his eyes full of love, and declared, "Woman, you have great faith! Your request is granted" (v. 28). Her daughter was immediately healed.

The story could have ended so differently. She could have walked away, angrily muttering something about Jesus being too busy for her. She could have started a blog bashing ministry leaders. But she didn't. She pursued him. She pressed in. She prayed harder. She chose to trust his character. And from some fractured place inside her heart, faith, with a frantic and reckless cry, broke through. His silence drew it out of her.

Great faith arose from great silence.

Faith is most authentic and dynamic when you are overcome by doubt but still choose to follow him.

And, like the Canaanite woman, there may be long stretches on the journey when we don't hear his voice. It's then that we have to trust. It's then that we have to go beyond what we just hear from him and accept what we know is true about him. Embracing who he is, not just who we want him to be. And whether we hear from him or not, he is still orchestrating something beautiful in our lives, quickening our senses, filling our hearts with anticipation, amplifying our awareness and longing for him.

» «

Let's take this idea deeper. What if, in the silence, God is still speaking, but in a different way?

What do I mean?

Well, let's go back to the phrase "the silence of God" and ask: Is God really ever silent? Or do we just perceive it that way?

You see, if we believe in the God of the Bible, by definition we believe in a God who endlessly speaks. Genesis begins with a cacophony of words cascading from the mouth of God:

"Let there be . . . let there be . . . let there be . . ."

And the worlds were made.

God spoke to Adam and Eve. He spoke to their descendants. He spoke to and through poets, prophets, priests, and kings. The gospel of John, which begins with a retelling of the Genesis narrative, tells us that "the Word became flesh and dwelt among us" (John 1:14 NKJV). If words reveal the heart of the speaker, then Jesus is what God sounds like. Hebrews 1:1–3 says,

In the past God spoke to our ancestors through the prophets at many times and in various ways, but in these last days he has spoken to us by his Son, whom he appointed heir of all things, and through whom also he made the universe. The Son is the radiance of God's glory . . . sustaining all things by his powerful word.

Notice that God's word sustains reality. The cosmos pulsates and throbs with it. Creation comes alive by it. There is not a single atom anywhere that isn't animated by him. And that includes the seven billion billion billion atoms that define you. You came to exist because of his word. And you continue to exist because of his word.

He is the God who speaks. He never withdraws. He never abandons. He is always near (see Psalm 139).

But, if that's true, then why does he seem so silent in my life? Why can't I hear him?

It's possible that he is truly silent. But I'm more inclined to think that the issue is less God's silence and more our inability to hear. If he sustains all things with his word, then we need a heart that is perceptive and aware, sensitized to the beauty and mystery of his voice.

Remember, God often speaks in ways we don't expect or even understand. I think of the prophet Elijah. In 1 Kings 19, he was desperate to hear the voice of God. He was being hunted by a demented and furious queen, Jezebel, who was hell-bent on seeing him killed. He ran into the wilderness, scrambled up the side of a mountain, and caught his breath inside a cave. He was exhausted. Suddenly, a strong wind blew, sending rocks tumbling below. Then an earthquake viciously ruptured the ground, followed by a fire that scorched everything in its path. After the dramatic display of power, there was something more. Something unexpected: "A still small voice . . . came to him" (1 Kings 19:12–13 NKJV).

A gentle blowing. A delicate whisper. And God spoke. To Elijah, his words were like cold water on a hot and dusty day.

Sometimes God speaks through the sensational and dramatic: wind, earthquakes, fire, turning a coffee run at Starbucks into a wedding. In those moments it's like God is shouting at us, daring us not to believe in him. But, most of the time, he doesn't speak that way. It's less a shout and more a whisper; it's sublime and faint, like a gentle breeze or an elegant dance.

The story is told of the famous performer Isadora Duncan. She was once asked if she could put into words what it was like to dance with such magnificence and grace. She replied, "If I could say it, I wouldn't have to dance it!"

To encounter God's voice is to join a dance. It defies words, it enhances words. It's beautiful, melodic, and entirely other. It comes to us in unexpected places, when we're huddled on the side of a mountain, sequestered and afraid, and it whispers, not in a wind, earthquake, or fire, but through a still small voice.

But hearing his voice is not enough. Hearing is just the simple act of perceiving sound. He wants us to listen. Listening is an art. It's focusing, waiting, breathing, watching, and being still.

Be still, and *then* you will know he is God. The only way I can hear the whisper of God is if I silence the noise around me and within me.

I don't know about you, but for me that is so hard to do. The Hebrew word for *wait* can be translated as "to twist or writhe in pain." Being still sometimes feels like agony. And the world we live in only makes it worse. We're inundated with noise. Our minds are fragmented by distraction. In America, we collectively check our phones eight billion times per day.[4] We're driven by the neurotic illusion of connectedness.

But if we want to stay connected to God, we have to figure out a way to build rhythms of solitude and rest into the cadence of our lives. We have to hit the pause button. He wants to speak to us. His heart is overflowing with love. The civil rights activist Maya Angelou said, "There is no greater agony than bearing an untold story inside you."[5] What if God's heart is aching with stories to share? What if there are insights, truths, perspectives, and encouragement just waiting for us, but we're too distracted to receive them?

Busyness is the enemy of love.

And if we want our relationship with God to thrive, not just survive, that may mean saying no to things, even good things, so that our love can grow.

» «

In Genesis 28 Jacob had a mysterious dream of a stairway, stretching from heaven to earth. He watched in awe as angels climbed up and down it. After he awoke, Jacob began to worship and exclaimed, "Surely the Lord is here, and I knew it not!" (v. 16).

I've always been slightly envious of people who have such lucid, meaningful dreams. Mine are the subconscious equivalent of postmodern art: often confused and really weird. I once dreamt that I was climbing the Himalayan mountains dressed, for some unknown reason, as a giant squid. I was knee-deep in snow, except I didn't have any knees. If any of you have an interpretation for that dream, let me know, because I don't have a clue.

But for Jacob, his dream was profound and the meaning undeniable: God was near. In fact, he was so close that Jacob didn't even realize it.

Sometimes the difficulty with experiencing God's presence isn't that he is so far away; it's that he is so close. He's like the air we breathe but don't notice. The poet Elizabeth Barrett Browning wrote,

> Earth's crammed with heaven
> And every common bush afire with God;
> But only he who sees, takes off his shoes.[6]

In Exodus 3, when God told Moses to take off his sandals, it was because he was standing on holy ground. How that must have surprised him! He knew that area of the desert well. He had walked on it for forty years as a shepherd. For Moses, it was where he worked. In his mind it was only common, dusty, dirty, sheep-trampled ground. But God said it was holy.

What if the ground you're on right now is soaked through with holiness? What if every detail of your life is permeated by the silhouette of God? What if the very atmosphere around you is infused by his voice?

God speaks. It just may not be in the way you're expecting.

- He speaks through other people. Even the ones who annoy you.
- He speaks through the arts: good books, music, poetry, songs, and photography.
- He can speak through dreams (just maybe not ones that involve squid).

- He speaks through creation, as we inhale the beauty of what he made.
- He speaks through conviction and the gnawing sense that something is wrong. (Sometimes the issue isn't God's silence but the deafening sound of sin. Sin wants to be the loudest voice in our life. Don't let it be.)
- He speaks through our pain.
- He speaks in our loss.
- He even speaks in our doubt.

If God exists, then there is no such thing as ordinary ground. It's all holy. This moment, right now, wherever you are, is holy. God invites you to take off your sandals and sink your toes in deep and worship.

He is here.

The fingerprints of God are all over your life.

>> <<

There were so many times in my life when I doubted God because I couldn't hear his voice. And there are times I still do. But I'm also learning to trust him even when I don't hear him.

I'm learning that God's silence isn't his absence.

I'm learning that God is found in ordinary things. And I'm learning that when I'm thirsty, and faltering through the canyons of faith, it's often God's way of calling me into greater spiritual growth. After all, the view is lovely on the mountain, but fruit grows in the valley.

A few years ago, Rutgers University did a study of trees in which they discovered that in times of rain, the roots remain relatively shallow. However, in seasons of drought, the roots go deeper. The tree presses them into the earth; in some cases they descend hundreds of feet, probing and seeking water.[7]

Like a tree, the roots of your soul are most deepened in seasons of thirst. Jesus taught, "Blessed are those who hunger and thirst for righteousness, for they will be filled" (Matthew 5:6). Silence is God's way of generating that thirst within you. As we saw in the story of the Canaanite woman, it's his catalyst to grow, mature, animate, and develop your faith.

Kierkegaard illustrated this with a story of a very rich king who fell in love with a beautiful maiden. His heart melted with desire for her. The only problem was, because of his wealth and influence, how would he ever know that she truly loved him in return?

She would say she loved him, of course, but would she truly? Or would she live with him in fear, nursing a private grief for the life she had left behind? Would she be happy at his side? How could he know for sure? If he rode to her forest cottage in his royal carriage, with an armed escort waving bright banners, that too would overwhelm her. He did not want a cringing subject. He wanted a lover, an equal. He wanted her to forget that he was a king and she a humble maiden and to let shared love cross the gulf between them. For it is only in love that the unequal can be made equal.[8]

And so, the king came up with a plan. One day, he approached her dressed as a beggar. His clothes were ragged and torn. He took on a new identity. He renounced his throne. He wanted her to love him for the sake of love, and only then would he know that her love was true.

The truest test of love isn't when love is easily obtained; it's when we have to seek it out. It's easy to love God when he's close, when his voice ricochets through our lives. But veracious love is born in seasons of silence. Why? Because it's in the asking, seeking, and knocking that we step past the doorway into intimacy. In the words of Mother Teresa,

> In the silence of the heart God speaks. If you face God in prayer and silence, God will speak to you. Then you will know that you are nothing. It is only when you realize your nothingness, your emptiness, that God can fill you with Himself. Souls of prayer are souls of great silence.[9]

When I first met Elyssa, God spoke in such a clear and undeniable way, probably because he knew I would mess it up if he didn't. On our first date, we talked for hours, shared stories, told jokes, let each other into our lives through words.

But now that we've been married for a while, I'm discovering that the magic of love isn't just found in words, but in silence too. There's a park near our house we love to explore. Often we walk together in silence. Neither one of us may be all that talkative, and yet we're still content. We can sit quietly over a meal, and through little gestures and subtle movements, I can understand what she is thinking. There are times when I know she's had a rough day. I get home, and one look says it all. Her eyes are full of language.

The longer I'm married to Elyssa, the more I'm realizing that, while words matter, what matters more is presence.

Could this be what C. S. Lewis had in mind when he prayed,

I know now, O Lord, why you utter no answer;
> You yourself are the answer.
> Before your face questions die away.
> What other answer would suffice?[10]

How I long to experience the depth of those words not just in marriage but in my journey of faith. To see God not just as some cosmic vending machine providing resolution for my doubt but as a friend. To be okay with silence. To let go of the relentless need to know and have all the answers and to be content, rooted in the tension of love.

And, my guess is, many of you thirst for that too; you ache for a relationship with God that's deeper than words. But until then, continue the journey of faith. And you will discover that trust is more beautiful than certainty, and his presence is the most eloquent language of all.

And who knows, when the journey is complete, maybe you'll be able to look back on all your doubt and say,

"You were there, and I knew it not."

Part III

Coming Home:

*Moving Through Doubt in
Pursuit of Deep Faith*

Chapter 9

The Luchador

God has hidden every precious thing in such a way that
it is a reward to the diligent, a prize to the earnest,
but a disappointment to the slothful soul. All nature is
arrayed against the lounger and the idler. The nut is
hidden in its thorny case; the pearl is buried beneath the
ocean waves; the gold is imprisoned in the rocky bosom
of the mountains; the gem is found only after you crush
the rock that encloses it; the very soil gives its harvests
as a reward of industry to the laboring husbandman.
So truth and God must be earnestly sought.
—A. B. SIMPSON

Whatever it takes.
—BRANDIN COOKS, NFL WIDE RECEIVER, LOS ANGELES RAMS

OVER THE LAST FOUR chapters, we've unpacked relevant issues that create doubt in our lives. We've grappled with thorny questions about Scripture, the interaction of science and faith, the world's suffering, and the silence of God. Of course, these issues are just the beginning. You may be experiencing doubts related to pluralism (what religions, if any, are true?), hypocrisy in the church, specific doctrines like heaven, hell, salvation, or the Bible's take on sexuality—the topics are endless. Whatever form of doubt it is, we need to realize that doubt is not a threat to our faith but an opportunity for renewed faith. Courageously confronting doubt is how we grow.

Now let's take it further and talk about practical ways that we can move through our doubt in pursuit of deep faith. Doubt creates space for myriad divergent outcomes. What you do with it makes all the difference. Doubt suppressed becomes toxic. But when it's dragged into the presence of God, it can become astonishingly beautiful and redemptive. We'll unpack what that looks like, then examine some nuts and bolts ways to live this out.

>> «

We last saw Jacob when he had a curious dream about ladders and angels (Genesis 28). It was an unforgettable and mystical moment. Following this, however, Jacob immediately stepped into a tragic period of loss, loneliness, broken relationships, disappointment, and intense confusion about his calling.

It's often like that, isn't it?

One day we have an encounter with God that's vivid and undeniable, and the next we question it all. By the time we reach Genesis 32, Jacob is consumed with doubt. The story reads:

> So Jacob was left alone, and a man wrestled with him till day-
> break. When the man saw that he could not overpower him, he

touched the socket of Jacob's hip so that his hip was wrenched as he wrestled with the man. Then the man said, "Let me go, for it is daybreak."

But Jacob replied, "I will not let you go unless you bless me."

The man asked him, "What is your name?"

"Jacob," he answered.

Then the man said, "Your name will no longer be Jacob, but Israel, because you have struggled with God and with humans and have overcome."

Jacob said, "Please tell me your name."

But he replied, "Why do you ask my name?" Then he blessed him there.

So Jacob called the place Peniel, saying, "It is because I saw God face to face, and yet my life was spared." The sun rose above him as he passed Peniel, and he was limping because of his hip. (Genesis 32:24–31)

This is the infamous story of the man who wrestled with God. Or, if you're a fan of the movie *Nacho Libre*, the world's first *luchador*. I've never been much of a wrestler. I once tried it in high school and hated it. Way too intimate. It's sweaty, smelly, slippery, and involves armpits. You find out all kinds of things about your opponent that can scar you for life.

It's fascinating to me that, of all the experiences Jacob could have had with God, it wasn't a handshake or a polite hug. It wasn't even a fist bump. Instead, God took him to the mat. How's that for an introduction? On top of that, it wasn't remotely close to a fair fight. It's tough wrestling with God, especially when he casually touches your hip and it rips out of socket. God is in the driver's seat here. For him, it was like wrestling with a toddler: the kid may fantasize he's a T. rex and about to eat you, but everyone knows who's calling the shots.

So why did God meet Jacob this way? Why all the drama and overtones of WWF? What's going on here?

Simply this: it's a story about Jacob's faith becoming his own.

Jacob grew up in a home that was staunchly loyal to God. His grandfather was Abraham, legendary for his faith, and his godly parents were Isaac and Rebecca. Jacob had heard breathtaking tales of God's power: how he called, led, provided for them, and rescued them from their enemies. He had personally seen God move in miraculous ways and had witnessed spectacular answers to prayer. Jacob trusted, loved, and believed in the God of his family.

But, still, it was not enough. God wanted to take Jacob deeper.

Jacob's name in Hebrew (בקעי) means "heel snatcher" or "supplanter." It's the English equivalent of scoundrel, fraud, or deceiver. Brutal. Could you imagine being at a party and having to introduce yourself that way? "Hey, I'm Scoundrel. Good to meet you." Talk about awkward. And, keep in mind, this was in a culture where an individual's name was everything. Back then, names revealed an individual's character and personality and even shaped their destiny. Today, we name our kids because we like how it sounds or because we think it's edgy. But back then, your name defined you. That's why Jacob's parents named his brother Esau (וְשֵׂע). Esau means "red" or "hairy." Because, well, that's what he was. The Bible's version of *Duck Dynasty*.

Everything about Jacob was the shocking antithesis of his brother. His brother was burly, bearded, and loved to hunt. He preferred his coffee strong and black. Jacob was "smooth skinned," artsy, and liked decaf with soy. They not only didn't understand each other; they hated each other. Jacob cheated and tricked his brother. He swindled his birthright for a bowl of soup. He even clothed himself in goatskin to impersonate Esau and steal his blessing. His blind father was confused: "You sound like Jacob, but your hands feel hairy like Esau's" (Genesis 27:22 CEV). Esau was justifiably furious, and, wisely, Jacob ran for his life.

Which brings us to Genesis 32. At this point, Jacob is full of doubt. Fear of his brother had driven him far from home, but his fraudulent past was quickly catching up with him. Jacob was intensely insecure, pretentious, and deceptive. But God perceived something more in him. Where Jacob only saw his failures, God saw potential—a future leader and a man of vibrant faith. It just needed to be unmasked. God had to strip away Jacob's façade and expose, humble, and change him once and for all.

They wrestled under the stars, and Jacob's strength was vanquished. His hip, thrown out of socket, burned; his body throbbed in pain. But even then, Jacob refused to abandon his grasp of God. Instead, he tightened his grip. "I will not let you go unless you bless me!"

Let's pause there.

Here in the West, at least in Christian subculture, the word *bless* has got to be the most overused word ever. It's the epitome of Christianese. Someone sneezes. "God bless you!" We open an email and it reads, "Bless you, brother!" I once overheard someone gossiping. The other person moaned: "I know. She's a terrible person, isn't she? . . . Bless her heart." As if that made it okay! We've turned *bless* into a tagline, a spiritual mantra, and in the process emptied it of substance. But in Hebrew culture, to bless someone was one of the most meaningful things you could do. The Jewish people believed that when you blessed someone, you were supernaturally releasing divine favor, grace, and shalom upon their life. That's why priests would end every gathering with a blessing, and it's why fathers, as they lay on their deathbeds, would whisper blessing over their children. To bless someone was to unleash the beauty and presence of God.

That's what Jacob was after. He was tired of running. He was sick of pretending. He wanted a life-defining collision with God.

"Bless me . . . Please, bless me."

And God did. He changed his name and, by doing so, transformed his character. No longer would he be called Jacob; his new name was Israel. Israel literally means "he who wrestles with God."

Jacob had wrestled with God and overcome. Not because God was defeated, but because Jacob was. Given a new name, Israel walked slowly away, hurting, limping, humbled, and renewed. He was never the same.

Yes, he still had doubts. Yes, he still struggled with faith, but something fundamental had shifted. Israel's faith had become his own. If you keep reading the story, he became the father of a great nation called Israel, a people who, like him, knew what it was like to wrestle with God in dark and lonely places. Rabbi Jonathan Sacks wrote, "Like Jacob wrestling with the angel . . . Jews refused to let go of God, and God refused to let go of them. They wrestle still. So do all who have faith."[1]

» «

The story of Jacob wrestling with God is a beautiful depiction of what deep faith looks like. Deep faith is an intimate, tenacious, all-of-life, sweaty, bloody, sometimes clumsy, and always real encounter with God. Faith isn't a choreographed script; it's a wrestling mat. It means taking all of your fears, sins, insecurities, and doubts and going head-to-head with God. And yes, you'll probably get bruised, broken, and lose your swag. But it's better to be an authentic mess before God than a fake religious person.

Faith means going all in.

If you want deep faith, not just the faith of your parents, friends, or church, but a faith that changes you and makes you come alive, then there is no other way. A faith that can't be tested can't be trusted.[2] In Galatians 6:16, Paul says that we are "the Israel of God." In other words, because our spiritual heritage is full of people who wrestled with God, then we are called to be wrestlers too.

The only way that the Jacob in us can become Israel, the only way our faith can grow, is if we bring all of who we are to God. Everything. And that includes our doubts. Especially our doubts. The British theologian Kallistos Ware said, "Faith implies not complacency but taking risks, not shutting ourselves off from the unknown but advancing boldly to meet it."[3]

Faith matures as it moves past the safe and predictable and into the dark, doubt-filled places. Faith refuses to reduce your dreams to the size of your fears. Faith doesn't hide from questions but passionately struggles with them. And Scripture is crowded with limping, screaming, sweaty *luchadors* who did just that:

- Moses wrestled with God on Sinai when Israel was about to be destroyed (Exodus 32). Then God revealed himself, and Moses saw his glory.
- Sarah, at the age of sixty-five, questioned, laughed, and lied when she heard God's promise to give her a son (Genesis 18:10–15).
- Habakkuk, whose name means "wrestler," went to the mat

with God in the ramparts; he contended with God over issues of faith, justice, mercy, and love (Habakkuk 1:2–4).

- Paul, pained with an unrelenting thorn in his flesh, cried out to God for healing (2 Corinthians 12:7–10).

Scripture doesn't tell the story of people who sluggishly tolerated doubt; it describes people who ruthlessly battled their doubts. They burned for something more than just a cursory, vapid, two-dimensional faith. Socrates noted, "The unexamined life is not worth living." The authors and heroes of the Bible insisted that the unexamined faith is not worth believing.

And so, chapter after chapter, verse after verse, they boldly, passionately, and audaciously wrestled with their God. Their ragged voices yelled, "I won't let you go until you bless me!" They knew it would be hard and harrowing, but it was worth every second.

» «

Elie Wiesel, who survived Auschwitz but whose faith nearly vanished in its smoke, recalled that his faith was "wounded" but stronger: "My tradition teaches that no heart is as whole as a broken heart, and I would say that no faith is as solid as a wounded faith."[4]

A wounded faith is anything but safe. It's not safe to wrestle with the hardest issues that challenge us. It's not safe to ask the questions that no one is asking. It's so much easier to remain complacent and listlessly embrace a comfortable, though boring, Christian life. The author Wilbur Rees once wrote,

I would like to buy $3.00 worth of God, please. Not enough to explode my soul or disturb my sleep, but just enough to equal a cup of warm milk or a snooze in the sunshine. I want ecstasy, not transformation; I want the warmth of the womb, not a new birth. I want a pound of the Eternal in a paper sack. I would like to buy $3.00 worth of God, please.[5]

That kind of posture toward God is the spiritual equivalent of a TV dinner. It's compartmentalized, requires very little effort, and is void of any real substance. It settles for Hallmark, skin-deep clichés rather than real relationship. It still experiences doubt, but isn't willing to bring them into the light. It demands instantaneous blessing from God, but isn't willing to wrestle with God. Three dollars' worth of God is worse than nothing, because it isn't real.

True Christianity, however, is less like a TV dinner and more like a wok bowl: faith and doubt are mixed together; it's chaotic, complicated, and more difficult to make. But it sure tastes good. Faith isn't about pushing buttons, it's about getting in the fire. Faith isn't about "inviting Jesus into your life," it's about stepping into his. Faith is when the real you surrenders to the real God. But when you hold back, he won't lead you forward.

God can't bless the fake you.

» «

In his book *Christianity Rediscovered*, Vincent Donovan recounts his missionary work among the Masai tribe in Eastern Africa.[6] After several years of learning and serving the Masai people, Vincent's faith hit a wall. He felt overwhelmed with doubt. He opened up and shared his struggles with one of the Masai elders who had become a close friend. Then the elder said something remarkable. He gently explained to him that in the Masai language there are two words for faith. One word means to agree with something, but it lacks passion, emotion, and struggle. He said that kind of faith was like a white hunter killing prey for sport. When he sees the animal, he merely holds up his rifle and pulls the trigger. He doesn't hear the animal breathe or feel its pain; it's all done from a safe and distant place.

The second word for faith, however, is much more intimate. The elder told Vincent that it was more like a lion hunting its prey. The lion longs and yearns for its prey; it thinks of nothing but capturing it. It tracks the prey through the long grass for hours, sometimes days. And then, when the lion senses the prey is near, it moves forward, its nose filled with its scent. With every fiber of muscle poised, the lion leaps out of the grass with a roar and enfolds the prey in its arms, making it a part of itself.

That, the elder said, is what deep faith looks like.

Knowing God is so much more than passionless acceptance, suppressing doubt with endless affirmations of songs and sermons, or blindly checking a religious box. Knowing God is pursuit. Anyone can pull a trigger. But deep faith means tracking God down, hill after hill, through unfamiliar, obscure terrain, until you see him. True faith, like love, won't be satisfied until it encounters the desire of its heart.

In 1 Corinthians 13:7, Paul wrote that love "believes all things, hopes all things, endures all things" (NKJV).

Love. Just. Won't. Quit.

Yes, you'll still doubt. But maybe you'll discover that loving and being loved by God makes all the doubt worth it.

» «

So what does this look like practically? How do we love God in this way? How do we wrestle like Jacob?

Most of us don't see God standing in our living room challenging us to a brawl! It's an interesting story but hard to wrap our minds around. Let's go back to Jacob wrestling on the mat. Notice the question that God asked him:

"What is your name?" (Genesis 32:27).

Why did God ask him this? Obviously he knew what Jacob's name was. You're not going to wrestle a person all night unless you have some unspoken history with them. Something else is going on here. Like so much in the Bible, there are layers of meaning that push us past the surface.

Here's what we uncover: God asked not for his sake but for Jacob's.

God wanted Jacob to own his name. He wanted him to stop pretending and open himself up to truth and grace. For years, Jacob had been living a life of deceit, running from God and others. He wasn't ready to come to terms with his Jacob-ness. So God called him out. God wanted Jacob to be honest about who he was, so he could make him into who he needed to be.

The same thing is true for you and me.

God wants to change us, refine us, and call us Israel, but that can only happen if we're willing to go to the mat and hold nothing back. That means having the guts to tell him our name.

It means being brutally honest about our doubts.

It means peeling off the mask to let him see who we really are. Jacob's name was the deepest part of him. Likewise, our doubts reside in the deepest part of us. God wants to draw them out.

It's impossible to wrestle with someone and not get

uncomfortably close. Within seconds, you'll feel their hot breath on your face, their muscles tensing around you, their veins pounding against your skin. Wrestling with God feels the same way. He wants you to experience his presence, skin against skin. He wants you to sweat, struggle, and strain. But, most of all, he wants you to be real.

If you're confused or offended by what you read in Scripture, don't just dismiss it or over-spiritualize it. Ask the tough questions. Tell him what you think. God can handle it!

If questions about science bother you, ask the One who invented it. Let him know your doubts and fears.

If you're struggling to understand why God allows suffering, don't repress it or act like it's not an issue, because it is. Like David in the Psalms, be open about your woundedness and the wounds of others. Don't be afraid to ask why.

If you're struggling with the silence of God, then don't settle for silence. Press in. Make some noise. Ask God to speak.

The only way superficial faith becomes genuine faith is by mouthing truth. It's when we wrestle, question, agonize, and shout. It's when we specifically name our fears, tears, and doubts. That's when we're set free.

Of course, this is just another way of describing prayer.

For many, the word *prayer* leaves them cold, because they think of hard pews and religious-sounding scripts. But true prayer is anything but that. It's not passive, heartless repetition; it's feisty, untamed, won't-take-no-for-an-answer wrestling with God. True prayer weeps, shouts, groans, and actively waits for God to show up. Prayer is speaking truth about and over our doubts. Prayer is the space of expectation between your doubts and God's healing.

According to the philosopher Peter Kreeft, "Prayer is a way of opening up your soul so that more of God can enter."[7]

That's why, in 1 Thessalonians 5:17, Paul urges us to "pray continually." When we pray, we are cutting a channel for God's healing to flow into our lives. But "continual" prayer is only possible if it's more than something we do; it must be something we are. Prayer like this is quietly rooted in each moment, breathing God's presence, in and out, waiting for him to speak.

So when you encounter doubt, breathe it out. Give it to God. Then ask him to fill you with himself. First Peter 5:7 says, "Cast all your anxiety on him because he cares for you."

All your anxiety.

That kind of prayer is deeper than authenticity; it's vulnerability. Authenticity says, "This is who I am. Accept me." Vulnerability says, "This is who I am. Change me." Vulnerability values transformation over affirmation. It means being candid about your innermost struggles. Praying like this matters because you may unearth things about your doubt that need to be addressed. Vulnerable prayer breaks the defensive shell to lay open what lies beneath. It may be that your doubt is simply an intellectual or emotional symptom of an unseen wound: disappointment with God, disillusionment with the church, something that happened in your childhood, unforgiveness, bitterness, an absent father, an emotionally distant mother, frustration with how life has turned out. These wounds can manifest themselves as doubt, and so we mistakenly assume that doubt is the issue, but in reality, doubt could be our soul's way of screaming out for healing, redemption, and renewal. Vulnerable prayer means giving God the space to patiently lead us to the place where healing can begin.

Have you ever shut your finger in a car door? It's surprising how painful that can be! Last time I did it, my thumb hurt so badly that I actually thought it had come off. I yanked it out of the closed door, and to my surprise it was still intact. But my feelings were not. Holding my mangled thumb, I immediately, uncontrollably, started jumping up and down by the side of the road. It looked like a Holy Spirit revival. I even kicked the tire with my foot. Not smart. The only thing I didn't do was speak in tongues. Thirty seconds into my dance, a car drove by— cautiously. It looked like someone was holding up a cell phone to the window. I can only imagine what they thought or posted online. #pastorthuglife

Prayer looks something like that.

Prayer is the moment when you let it all out and you don't care who is watching. Prayer is the shameless, outrageous, flagrant dance of a wounded soul.

In his magisterial book *A Secular Age*, the sociologist Charles Taylor uses the words *porous* and *buffered* to differentiate between forms of cultural selves.[8] He makes the argument that in recent centuries we've slowly become closed to the presence of the divine in our lives. We're a lot less open than we think we are. I think the same language applies to prayer. A "buffered" self sees itself as impenetrable; it's resistant to the intervention of God. On the other hand, a "porous" self lives in hope-filled vulnerability. It leaks honesty and absorbs grace.

That's who God wants us to be.

We encounter God not when our hearts are buffered, unyielding, and proud, but when we remove all barriers and let him in. We feel him when we relinquish our hearts like defenseless sponges and let him squeeze. And, of course, that can hurt. A lot. But it's essential if we want to be made whole. Jesus said, "Come to me, all you who are weary and burdened, and I will give you rest" (Matthew 11:28).

When we hear the word *rest*, what so often comes to mind is inactivity, passivity, or sleeping in on Saturday morning. But the word for *rest* that Jesus used is substantially different. It's not passive; it's active. It speaks of interaction, relationship, and a heart captivated by God.

This kind of rest is miles away from indifference—and even farther away from the self-assured confidence that all your doubts are happily and neatly resolved. In fact, when you come to Jesus, chances are you'll still carry your doubts and leave with them too.

And most likely, you'll walk with a limp.

You'll still have the same questions but with one significant change: you'll be transformed because you've wrestled with God. You've encountered him in new and intimate ways. And because of that, you're not the same person that you used to be. You're both at rest and profoundly restless. You've died and come alive. And now you only want more of him.

» «

Pray your doubts. Be honest. Be vulnerable. Be persistent. Like Jacob, wrestle all night if you have to. Track God down. Be courageous. Boldly approach his throne of grace. James 5:16 says, "The earnest prayer of a righteous person has great power and produces wonderful results" (NLT). What is an earnest prayer? *Earnest* and *energy* have the same root. So when you pray earnestly, it's like a current of electricity surging into a light bulb. Prayer is the defeat of mediocrity in the name of hope.

But this raises a vital question.

What about those times when our energy is spent and we're too fatigued to pursue him? What if the light has gone out in our hearts? What can we do if we're too discouraged and overwhelmed to even think about wrestling God?

Here's the good news: God meets us anyway.

In Jacob's story, it wasn't Jacob chasing after God; God chased after him. God pursued him. God relentlessly tracked him down. God never, ever gave up on him.

You might be in a place right now where it feels like your faith has failed. You're depleted, and your doubts have led you far from home. Maybe you've forgotten what home looks like. Maybe the little faith that you have is hanging on by a thread.

Or maybe you've already let go.

Listen. You need to know this: God has not let go of you.

He has not turned his back on you, he has not given up on you, he has not walked away. In fact, if anything, he's closer now than ever before.

» «

Let's return to the conversation between Vincent Donovan and the Masai elder. Vincent learned that faith, like a predatory lion, is a ravenous pursuit. Vincent was amazed and encouraged by these words. But his friend wasn't done yet. He continued,

> We did not seek you out, Padri. We did not even want you to come to us. You searched us out. You followed us away from your house into the bush . . . into our villages, our homes. You told us of the High God, how we must search for him, even

leave our land and our people to find him. But we have not done this. . . . We have not searched for him. He has searched for us. He has searched us out and found us.[9]

And then, after a moment's silence, the elder whispered, "All the time we think we are the lion. In the end, the lion is God."

Chapter 10

Be the Answer

*Every day God invites us on the same kind of adventure.
It's not a trip where He sends us a rigid itinerary, He
simply invites us. God asks what it is He's made us to
love, what it is that captures our attention, what feeds
that deep indescribable need of our souls to experience
the richness of the world He made. And then, leaning
over us, He whispers, "Let's go do that together."*
—Bob Goff

Come, follow me.
—Jesus

MOVING THROUGH OUR DOUBT is about the small things.
Small steps, disciplines, decisions, and acts of trust that gradually
accumulate into something beautiful. Eugene Peterson describes it
as a "long obedience in the same direction."[1] In an age of instant
gratification, this grates on us. We're not prepared for a time-
consuming journey. We prefer shortcuts over patient endurance. I
can relate to the words of an old Jewish prayer, "Give me patience,

now!" But when Jesus calls us to follow him, it means switching to the slow lane.

Recently I attended a wedding that was the stuff dreams are made of. It was perfect. Everything—the picturesque outdoor setting, the weather, décor, music, reception, and especially the joy—made it unforgettable. I kept waiting for a unicorn to appear. But for me, the most memorable moment happened just as the ceremony began. The music dramatically started, and everyone rose as the bride moved gracefully down the aisle. She was stunning. Everyone looked on; the awestruck groom was fighting a losing battle with tears. As she slowly walked by, a little boy who was standing next to me was utterly mesmerized. He was no older than three. As she passed, he suddenly yanked on his dad's arm and, in a super loud voice, declared, "Daddy! I want to marry a girl!" What's funny is that it wasn't even a request. It was an announcement. In his mind, it wasn't up for debate. He was ready to settle down.

For many of us, that's how we approach our spiritual life. At least it is for me. Forming a relationship is long, hard work; it requires all of us, demands our time, affection, and attention. We'd much rather move past the formalities and, like Humperdinck in *The Princess Bride*, "skip to the end."

I often think about that as it relates to doubt. If God wanted to, he could resolve all our doubts instantaneously; he could snap his finger, put a ring on ours, and escort us to heaven. But he doesn't. For some reason, he calls us on a journey, not just to attend a ceremony. He takes us the long way home, and I think the reason is because God values intimacy over resolution. He wants us to know him, not just know about him. Belief in God looks more like trust than certainty, because trust is the language of relationships.

And so, God invites us to trust him in all seasons. Not only through enchanting mountains where faith is as natural as breathing, but when he leads us into long, desolate valleys, where doubts squeeze the life from our soul.

In the previous chapter, we heard the story of Jacob, a man who experienced doubt but also chose to trust. He wrestled with God all night, refusing to let go until God changed his name.

We saw that prayer is a practical way that we can wrestle too.

In this chapter, I want to go deeper and look at three more ways we can wrestle with God through our doubts.

None of these are easy, quick-fix answers. They take time, effort, and resolve. But if you stick with it, you may discover that your name is changed too.

Let's start with one of the most vital: a commitment to learn.

» «

One of the tragic ideas of our age is that many people define faith as "belief without evidence." This implies faith is essentially a renunciation of rationality, or, as Sigmund Freud believed, an attempt to evade the inescapable bleakness of life. The atheist Richard Dawkins concurs: "Faith is an evil precisely because it requires no justification and brooks no argument."[2] This is disturbing on a number of levels. First of all, it fails to address Dawkins's own faith in a godless universe, but even more sinister, it suggests that if you want to be a Christian, you have to check your brain at the door.

Wrong.

Apprenticeship to Jesus is a holistic, all-of-life endeavor. This includes not only our spiritual life but our intellectual life too. Sometimes we bifurcate spirituality and reason and assume they operate in different spheres. But in Scripture, the two are inexorably woven together. Reason and worship draw from one another; they give each other life. Romans 12:2 defines worship as a transformation and "renewing of your mind."

When Jesus called his disciples, he was inviting them into a life where their hearts, souls, minds, and strength were all fully engaged (Luke 10:27). How we think is a profoundly sacred and loving act.

Thought is worship.

That is why Jesus spent so much time teaching his disciples. He endlessly tilled the soils of Scripture, overturning their prejudice and paradigms, lavishly planting kingdom seeds in their hearts; he watered them with truth. Mark 4:2 says, "He taught them many things." Of the ninety times that Jesus was addressed in the Bible, sixty times he was called "teacher." The theologian and professor Keith Ferdinando calls Jesus a "theological educator" and wrote,

> He cultivated an atmosphere which expected and welcomed questions, discussion, and debate. His purpose was not simply to impart content . . . more than that, he wanted to engage their intelligence and have them wrestle with the issues which arose in the course of ministry.[3]

Jesus believed there was an unremitting synergy between the life of the mind and all-in devotion to God. So did everyone who followed him. The early church was committed to learning (Acts 2:42). Paul crafted intellectual arguments as he presented the case for faith (Acts 17:16–34). Later, he encouraged Timothy to study and make every effort to correctly handle the Word of God (2 Timothy 2:15). For centuries, Christians worshipped with their hearts *and* their minds. That is why, historically, Christians have been pioneers in education, founding centers of learning throughout the world.

Our ancestors believed reason was not the enemy of faith but the fuel of faith. They concluded that what we think—and how we think—matters. An old proverb warns,

> Be careful of your thoughts, for your thoughts become your words. Be careful of your words, for your words become your actions. Be careful of your actions, for your actions become your habits. Be careful of your habits, for your habits become your character. Be careful of your character, for your character becomes your destiny.

How we think inevitably shapes who we become.

Let's think about that in terms of doubt. Doubt loves to stay in the shadows. It's secretive and reclusive. It gnaws and lingers in the recesses of our minds, subtly influencing our thought life. Unaddressed, doubt can become toxic, curdling like old milk, poisoning our passion and thirst for truth.

So how do we drag doubt into the light? By addressing it head-on. And that means committing ourselves to learn.

If you're struggling with a specific doubt about God, confront it. Research. Ask questions. Grab coffee with your pastor. Read a good book. Download a podcast. Enroll in a class. Talk to a professor. Unearth it, examine it, pull it apart. Just like Jacob wrestled with God, wrestle with your doubt.

Here's why this is so important. Some doubts can be resolved when we simply take the time to understand them more. An ancient Chinese proverb says, "Put a green branch in your heart, and the singing bird will come." In other words, do the hard work to put yourself in a place where the truth can find you. Learn. Inquire. Explore. Sometimes the answer will come, and sometimes you'll be birdless. But either way, you'll be changed in the process.

The worst thing we can do on the journey of faith is stagnate. According to the poet Alexander Pope,

> A little learning is a dangerous thing;
> Drink deep, or taste not the Pierian spring.[4]

If you have questions about Scripture, don't listlessly set them aside and hope the answer will magically appear. Drink deep from the well. Tear into the story. Pick up a good commentary or concordance. Go to the mat with God.

If you're drawn to atheism and have doubts about the existence of God, don't just read half of *The God Delusion* and then announce to your friends you've abandoned your faith. Go all in. Read, study, learn. Read books on both sides. Don't settle for the low-hanging fruit; instead, reach for the best arguments and fight it out.

If your faith is being shaken by the suffering you see, don't be content with cheesy Christian truisms or Facebook clichés. Cat posters won't cut it when you're face-to-face with cancer, disease, violence, or injustice. Lean into the chaos. Cry out to God. Talk to people who have gone through pain and have come out on the other side awash with hope. Immerse yourself in Scripture's lament and redemption. Dare to say, "I will not let you go until you bless me."

Eugene Peterson also said, "Pain entered into, accepted, and owned can become poetry."[5] That's what God wants to do with your doubt. Your doubts can diminish you, or they can push you into a bolder, richer, more vulnerable and resilient faith. Doubts are both an obstacle and an opportunity. When you commit to learn, you're making your doubts work for you rather than against you.

Remember, how you think shapes your destiny.

That's why, when Jesus chose his disciples, he relentlessly and passionately taught them. He laid an intellectual foundation they could build upon for years. He took them deep into the life of the mind so they could go far on the road of faith. He said, "Take my yoke upon you and learn from me" (Matthew 11:29). In the ancient world, a rabbi's yoke was his set of teachings, theology, and interpretation of Torah. Jesus was inviting them into a robust and flourishing intellectual journey.

That's the journey he invites us on as well. Every step of the way is an opportunity to learn. We should celebrate truth, wherever it is found. Notice, however, that when Jesus taught his disciples, he didn't teach them alone. He did it in community.

Which brings us to another practical way we can wrestle with God through our doubts: community.

» «

It's impossible to read the Bible and not realize faith's journey is meant to be done together. The idea is everywhere. The Bible begins with a triune God creating our world. He planted a garden and put a family inside. He then called Israel to be a community of hope for all people. In the New Testament, the church first began as a community of 12, which then grew to 120, then 3,000. They lived out their faith together. If you spend time in the Gospels and Epistles, you'll notice they're immersed in the language of community. In fact, fifty-nine times the phrase "one another" is found. Here are ten of them:

- Love one another. (John 15:17)
- Be devoted to one another. (Romans 12:10)
- Live in harmony with one another. (Romans 12:16)
- Serve one another. (Galatians 5:13)
- Be kind and compassionate to one another. (Ephesians 4:32)
- Submit to one another. (Ephesians 5:21)
- Forgive one another. (Colossians 3:13)
- Encourage one another. (1 Thessalonians 4:18)
- Do not slander one another. (James 4:11)
- Pray for one another. (James 5:16)

These "one anothers" were written during a time when Gnostic philosophy was mainstream. Gnosticism consisted of belief in gods who were distant and disinterested, and if you wanted to know them it required personal, secretive effort. Truth, it was maintained, isn't discovered in community, but isolation.

The writers of the New Testament, however, turned that narrative on its head. They taught that even as God is community, he has created us for community. They insisted that when you became a follower of Jesus, you weren't just brought out of your old life, you were welcomed into a new family. Hebrews 12:1–2 puts it this way: "Let us run with perseverance the race marked out for us, fixing our eyes on Jesus, the pioneer and perfecter of faith."

Notice the language the author used: Let us run. The race marked for us. Fixing our eyes. It's the language of togetherness. The race of faith (and doubt) wasn't meant to be run alone.

For most of us, however, this is a huge paradigm shift.

Sociologists say we live in an age of "radical individualism." In other words, we no longer see ourselves as part of a larger narrative, but curators of our own self-expression. It's a new form of

Gnosticism. A recent article in *Psychology Today* describes us as the "I" generation,[6] and our values have correspondingly shifted to accommodate this. We value autonomy over accountability and individual happiness over the greater good. We value "tolerance" over love because love is willing to challenge, whereas tolerance merely accepts. We value fierce independence over friendship. There was a time when a "friend" was someone you did life with, who walked beside you and knew you well. But now we've digitized relationships, creating unending superficial connections. And if we don't like someone? Easy. Just click "unfriend."

Unfortunately, we've carried this illusion of intimacy into the church. For many, "church" is something to consume rather than a family to invest in. "Worship" is a pseudo-media event rather than communal surrender to a loving God. Even reading Scripture has become individualistic: every verse filtered through the lens of "how does it speak to me?" rather than active participation in an historic, unfolding, we're-all-in-this-together story.

Is it any wonder that when we experience doubt, we don't know where to go? We're so used to flash-mob church—show up for an event, be entertained, and then leave—that we have no space to engage life's toughest questions. Doubt is too time-consuming, relationally complex, and spiritually exhausting.

The tragedy, however, is that when people leave the church, many don't come back. In his book *You Lost Me*, David Kinnaman argues that, because many of our churches aren't willing to engage with the difficult issues of doubt, we've alienated those who are hungry for deeper faith. He writes,

A generation of young Christians believes that the churches in which they were raised are not safe and hospitable places to express doubts. Many feel that they have been offered slick or half-baked answers to their thorny, honest questions, and . . . that the institutional church has failed them.[7]

This is not the way it was meant to be. God's heart is, and always has been, for the church to live as family. Church is where we wrestle, wonder, worship, and doubt together. Church is where we come with all the shrapnel of our past and find healing, acceptance, and grace. Church is where broken people discover they are not alone. That was God's vision when he first poured out his Spirit on the church in Acts 2. And that is God's vision for you.

It's true many churches haven't done a great job achieving this vision. It's true there's a ton that needs to change, but you can be the change.

You are the church.

Church isn't a building but a community of people who together pursue the way of Jesus. This means leaning into everything that is good, beautiful, and messy about our faith—and each other. It means struggling hand in hand through our doubts.

In Matthew 26, just hours before his death, Jesus sat around a table with friends. They sang. They prayed. He took a loaf of bread and broke it; he took a cup of wine and shared it. He said, "This is my body; this is my blood. Eat and drink in remembrance of me." Around the table sat a diverse group of people with serious issues, doubts, flaws, and struggles with faith.

But Jesus welcomed them all. He shared his broken body with them. He offered them a place at the table.

Where is that community for you? Who are the people around your table that you let into the secluded places of your life? In what ways can you share your brokenness with them?

You don't have to endure doubt alone.

You're part of a larger story. You're adopted into a big, gawky, dysfunctional, wonderful family called the church. You're the bride of Christ. You're the body of Christ. You're his hands and feet in the world. You might think, *but I don't like church because it's full of hypocrites.* True. But there is always room for one more! Church is a beautiful mess. It's where our imperfect faith is on display. But then we see Jesus, and mercy and healing begins. First Corinthians 12:26 says, "If one part suffers, every part suffers with it." When you doubt, you suffer. Sometimes, like Jacob, your hip gets thrown out of joint. You can try and hide it, sit at the table faking a smile and pretending everything's okay. But that's not why the table is there. The table represents naked, raw vulnerability: crucifixion, death, burial. It also represents resurrection and the possibility of restored faith.

Author Anne Lamott reveals that when the ancient Chinese cracked a valuable dish or jar, rather than throwing it away, they would adorn it with a gold leaf.[8] This wasn't done to hide the break but to draw attention to it. It was their way of saying, "We're not going to pretend this brokenness doesn't exist; instead, we're going to own it, share it, and turn it into something beautiful."

That's what Christian community should look like. It's unvarnished vulnerability, without masks and pretense. It's being honest with the real and wounded you and then allowing yourself to be adorned with grace. It's the liberating choice to let people see you at your worst, so they can see God at his best. It's sitting at a table with your closest friends, bound by thick ties of love, eating and drinking and sharing faith and doubt.

Christian community is broken bread. It's poured-out wine. And it's searching together for resurrection. In that space, doubt can become a source of faith; our limp, a dance; our lament, a song of hope.

If you are struggling with doubt, you need to be in community.

And this isn't just for your sake; it's for the sake of others. Even if you're not struggling with doubt, it's likely people near you are. They need you. They ache for your prayers, listening ear, and encouragement. The word *encourage* literally means "to give courage." You have the power to share courage with someone who is languishing in their faith. One of the most empowering things you can say to a friend who is doubting is, "I will love you through this." They need you. They need your presence. They need your strength. And they need your wounds too. Henri Nouwen wrote,

> Nobody escapes being wounded. We are all wounded people, whether physically, emotionally, mentally, or spiritually. The main question is not, "How can we hide our wounds?" so we don't have to be embarrassed, but "How can we put our woundedness in the service of others?" When our wounds cease to be a source of shame, and become a source of healing, we have become wounded healers.[9]

When Jesus sat at the table with his friends, the most infamous doubter in history was sitting with him. Someone somewhere (it wasn't Jesus) gave him the nickname "Doubting Thomas," and the name has stuck. In John 20, after Jesus rose again, Thomas struggled to believe.

You can't blame him.

I have a hard enough time believing that God will take away a headache, let alone raise someone from the dead. But still, Jesus didn't give up on him. He didn't judge him for his lack of faith.

Instead, he invited him to touch his wounds. Why did Jesus do this? Because he knew that his wounds were evidence of atoning love and a wellspring of healing for those whose faith faltered. Jesus' vulnerability was the initiation of Thomas's renewed faith. And so it is for anyone who is willing to share their wounds.

Your hurt can be someone else's hope.

Your story of doubt can be someone else's source of faith.

St. Francis of Assisi said, "We have been called to heal wounds, to unite what has fallen apart, and to bring home those who have lost their way."[10]

Which leads me to the final point I'd like to make in this chapter.

You can be the answer to your doubts.

» «

In Mark 9, a man ran to Jesus and collapsed headlong at his feet. He was anxious, broken, and in need of a miracle. He implored Jesus to heal his son. Jesus answered, "Everything is possible for one who believes" (v. 23).

In that moment, the man was confronted with the tension of belief and unbelief, faith and doubt, hope and despair. He intensely wanted to believe, wanted to imagine that everything would be okay, but at the same time he couldn't escape the reality of his story.

His son was sick, and he was out of options. It had been years. He had prayed thousands of times. He had cried out to God in the sanctuary. He had wept on the temple floor. But no answer. The heavens were silent.

Where was God?

And then, suddenly, God was standing before him. Flesh and blood. Grace and truth. The Word spoke: "Everything is possible for one who believes."

Jesus' words struck him in the deepest way. It exposed the wound. His heart was fragile, defenseless, ravaged by the agony of hope that only the truly broken can understand.

He caught his breath. His tears splashed on the ground. Did he still believe? Could he still believe?

And then he said it: "Lord, I believe; help my unbelief."

Of all the stories in the Bible, this has always struck me as unspeakably profound.

First of all, the man had a raw and vulnerable faith. Not the kind of faith that simply sounds spiritual or impressive, a wordy stream of silky platitudes or trite mystical phrases. His was the kind of faith that could only come from a place of desperation. He had tried all options, knocked on countless doors, unearthed every stone; he had nowhere left to go.

It was a faith born of anguish.

He genuinely believed that Jesus could do all things. Like a candle illuminating a room, his faith gave him vision when all was dark. It gave him a purpose, a reason to keep holding on.

Lord, I believe!

But then he said, "Help my unbelief."

Unbelief is more insidious and destructive than doubt. It's when doubt goes wrong. But this man couldn't hide from it anymore. He wouldn't pretend it wasn't there. Years of pain and unanswered prayers had forced him to acknowledge not just the light but the dark. He had to be honest. He had to be real. And so he brought it all to Jesus.

The faith and doubt.

The hope and despair.

The strength and weakness.

Lord, I believe. Help my unbelief.

And Jesus heard him. He didn't send him away, lecture him for his less-than-perfect faith. He answered his prayer, stepped into the brokenness, and healed his troubled son.

I love this story because it's a reminder that sometimes the best prayers are the messiest. Prayers that weep, worry, and worship. Prayers that scream, sigh, and sing. Prayers that reflect the entangled, complicated mess of everything we believe and doubt. And when words fail, and the best we can do is whisper, "Lord, I believe. Help my unbelief," still, God meets us there.

But it's also a reminder that the best prayers are lived out. This was a man racked with doubt. But he still chose to get up early that morning, find Jesus, and lay his son at his feet. He did something about his doubt. He held nothing back. Like Jacob, he dug in his heels. He was tenacious, determined, and tirelessly resolute. He refused to leave the same way he came in.

I want to suggest we do the same thing with our doubts.

There is a time to struggle, internalize, and process our doubts. There is a time to go deep within ourselves and analyze what we believe and why. There is a time for lament. There is a time to lock ourselves away like Habakkuk and say, "I'm not leaving until you give me the answer."

But there is also a time to stand up and *be* the answer.

In chapter 8 we explored the idea of judo theology. At the cross, Jesus took all the Enemy meant for evil, and he turned it into something good. As he died, he wrestled with penetrating questions about the silence of God: "Why have you forsaken me?" But he didn't let doubt win. Instead, through ragged breath, the

Forsaken One refused to forsake the world. He gave everything he had. His arms were stretched out. His body burned. His voice broke: "Father, forgive them, for they know not what they do."

What I'm saying is that doubt can be redeemed.

Mother Teresa promised, "Give yourself fully to God. He will use you to accomplish great things on the condition that you believe much more in His love than in your own weakness."[11] That's incredibly beautiful. Here was a woman who had stabbing doubts about why God was silent, but rather than allowing it to embitter and sabotage her faith, her doubt became the spark that fueled her mission to the world.

Redeemed doubt has the life-giving potential to ignite our faith. When we abandon our quest for certainty and choose instead to embrace the wonder and mystery of relationship, joy—like a luminous, healing flame—burns through the ruins of despair.

Maybe you're troubled by God's silence. I am too. What would it look like for you to be God's voice to others? To speak hope, life, and healing into places that know nothing but injustice and fear? Your words have inexhaustible potential to transform, convict, affirm, and inspire. Words create worlds.

Maybe you're struggling with doubts about the Bible. You look at it, and there are so many things that confuse and disturb you. Maybe it raises more questions than answers. What if, instead of dwelling on what you don't understand, you took what you *do* understand and lived into that? What matters to God is not just what you believe about the Bible, but what you do with it. Jesus said, "Love one another." That should keep us busy for a long time.

Maybe you're doubting God's goodness, because you can't understand why he'd allow something as evil as human trafficking, racism, sexism, or poverty. What would it look like for you to push against it and overcome evil with good? Dietrich Bonhoeffer wrote, "We are not to simply bandage the wounds of victims beneath the wheels of injustice, we are to drive a spoke into the wheel itself."[12]

When injustice causes you to doubt God's goodness or power, don't just internalize it and silently drift from him. Use that doubt to be a force for change. Drive yourself into the wheel of injustice. You are God's hands and feet. You are his image to a lost and lonely world.

If following Jesus doesn't lead you to the wounded and broken, then you're not following Jesus. His heart bends toward the marginalized. He fights for the victim, elevates the oppressed, and gives the voiceless a song.

Jesus runs to the people we run from.

Sometimes I wonder if God allows us to doubt in order to enlarge our hearts for the spiritually dispossessed. Think about it. If we had 100 percent certainty in our faith, if we could see God with perfect clarity, if every moment welcomed his presence, we probably wouldn't want to do anything else but live in that. It would be heaven, really. But what if doubt is just the discomfort we need to get out of the Holy of Holies and into a world that's struggling to believe?

The crucial difference between toxic doubt and redeemed, light-bearing doubt is love.

Redeemed doubt still has questions, but it endlessly moves beyond itself and looks for creative, faith-building ways to serve people with radical love. Toxic doubt is narcissistic and bends in on itself. It loves to be the cynic, refuses to be the healer.

Redeemed doubt takes the long way home, moving slowly

through the world because love takes time. Toxic doubt demands easy answers and shortcuts; it idolizes certainty but rejects mystery.

Redeemed doubt pushes through the crowd just to lay a child at Jesus' feet.

Redeemed doubt limps away from a night of wrestling with a new name and a message to share.

Redeemed doubt asks, what are the broken places that Jesus is weeping over and what would it look like to be his healing presence there?

A. W. Tozer said, "A scared world needs a fearless church."[13] Our world aches for hope. It longs to see what true faith looks like. It groans for the day when all things are made new.

As followers of Jesus we believe that will someday become reality. But until then, let's step into the world, praying, learning, and wrestling together.

And let's be the answer to our doubts.

Chapter 11

Balloons and Spears

> *To live within limits. To want one thing. Or a few*
> *things very much and love them dearly. Cling to them,*
> *survey them from every angle. Become one with them—*
> *that is what makes the poet, the artist, the human being.*
> —JOHANN WOLFGANG VON GOETHE

> *One thing I ask from the LORD, this only do I seek:*
> *that I may dwell in the house of the LORD all the*
> *days of my life, to gaze on the beauty of the LORD.*
> —PSALM 27:4

IN HIS ADVENTUROUS BOOK *Mysterious Island,* Jules Verne described the saga of five prisoners and a dog who together escaped from prison by hijacking a hot air balloon. It's an incredible story. The balloon traveled hundreds of miles east, encountered a colossal storm, and began dropping perilously 1,600 miles east of New Zealand. They had very little control of the balloon's direction and could only hope and pray that it brought them near to land. As they plunged down, however, they realized to their horror that they were surrounded by "a vast water desert of the Pacific."

In a desperate attempt to gain altitude, they immediately began to throw things overboard:

"Are we rising again?"

"No. On the contrary."

"Are we descending?"

"Worse than that, captain! We are falling!"

"For Heaven's sake heave out the ballast!"

"There! The last sack is empty!"

"Does the balloon rise?"

"No!"

"I hear a noise like the dashing of waves. . . . It cannot be more than 500 feet from us!"

"Overboard with every weight! . . . everything!"[1]

This continued for several days. The balloon dipped, then bounced back up as they found more things to throw off the sides. Ammunition, food, gold, provisions.

At last, there was nothing else to get rid of.

"The men had done all that men could do. No human efforts could save them now. . . . At four o'clock the balloon was only 500 feet above the surface of the water."[2]

As the balloon got closer and closer to the waves, their fear heightened. They could see the ocean below; it was surging, swelling, pulling them into a watery grave. It looked hopeless. But at the last moment, someone had an idea. In a final act of desperation, they stretched their hands up and clung to the ropes that were fastened to the balloon's basket. They held on for dear life. Then, with a sharp knife, one of the prisoners reached down and cut the basket free.

It was just the lift they needed. The balloon rose slightly into the air, the wind blew them farther east, and they eventually landed on the sandy shore of a "mysterious island."

>> <<

Life is an endless journey of letting go.

From the moment we're born, we're violently propelled into a world of change. Every day is a swirling, moving storm, a conflation of emotion, experience, memories, and relationships. Nothing ever stays the same. The ancient Greek philosopher Heraclitus said we do not step into the same river twice. The river moves on, and so does everything and everyone. Time slips through our fingers; the balloon descends. Like the castaways in Verne's novel, we're all trying to get home. And if we want to get there, sometimes we have to make torturous decisions about what to keep and what to let go.

Kierkegaard wrote, "Purity of heart is to will one thing."[3] The one thing is the rope that hangs from the balloon. It's what you cling to when everything else has been thrown off the side. It's that which remains.

What is your one thing?

If you've been on the journey of faith long enough, you know by now that the one thing is Jesus. He is the rope that holds everything, including us, together. Colossians 1:16–17 says,

For in him all things were created: things in heaven and on earth, visible and invisible, whether thrones or powers or rulers

or authorities; all things have been created through him and
him. He is before all things, and in him all things hold toget.....

Everything revolves around Jesus. He started us on the journey,
and he will be there when it's over. He is the source and satisfaction
of our deepest longing, the author and the finisher of our faith
(Hebrews 12:2). The story begins and ends with him. And if that's
true, then following him means letting go of whatever keeps us
from knowing him more.

The disciples abandoned their nets. The prisoners cut their
basket. Likewise, faith is about release and embrace. God is a
minimalist, and we should be too. We release the unnecessary to
embrace the essential. It's a slow and painful process, but it's how
we get home.

Less is best.

And that is what makes doubt such a vital part of the journey.
Doubt can help us discover what the One Thing is.

>> <<

When we doubt, it's like being stuck in the middle of a storm, in a
balloon, hundreds of feet above a raging sea. It's terrifying and disorienting. Our eyes anxiously scan the basket as we try to figure out
ways to keep the balloon up. As we saw in the last few chapters, this
means adopting practices such as prayer, community, learning, and
doing. But it also means taking time to assess what's on board and to
ask honest and probing questions about what's central to our faith.

This unmasks one of the benefits of doubt: it urges us to
rethink everything. It refines us. Doubt asks, "Do I really need
this? Or is it pulling me down? Is this question or issue really that

important? Can I live without it?" Doubt sifts through the baggage of our souls in search of truth.

Sometimes we may realize we've taken on things that we once thought were indispensable but have since become dead weight. During my season of doubt in Oxford, I experienced this. As I began to seriously reevaluate cherished beliefs, I unearthed beliefs that I mistakenly thought were essential but were not. For example, I had very specific views about creation and Bible prophecy that I had absorbed over the years, and I accepted them without question. I had synthesized them so deeply into my faith I assumed they were nonnegotiable. But, as I began to probe and examine, I recognized not only were my views probably wrong, they weren't as important as I thought they were. Doubt, like shears, began to prune my faith. It was an exhilarating, challenging, and exhausting process. But if I wanted to grow, I first had to cut back.

I'm not saying specific beliefs aren't important. For example, having orthodox views about God, the trinity, incarnation, sin, and salvation really matter! And if we throw those out, it wouldn't look like Christianity at all. What I am saying is that some of our beliefs may not be as essential as we think. The early church used the language of "open hand, closed fist." Some doctrines, they taught, were essential. We should hold on to those tightly. Others, however, are more negotiable and up for debate.

Sometimes our fists close over practices and beliefs that we think are essential, but if we look closer, they may just be the byproducts of history, tradition, social trends, personal bias, denominations, sermons, church splits, popular books, or Twitter posts. We're all a convoluted, conflated, complicated byproduct of our cultural moment. We know less than we think.

One benefit of doubt is that it teaches us to unclench our fists and evaluate truth. It asks, "Is this what the gospel is all about? Is this essential to my faith? Is this what Jesus had in mind? Is this worth fighting over?"

In World War II, at the Battle of La Ciotat, the Americans dropped hundreds of fake paratroopers near German troops. They wanted the Germans to divert all their efforts to taking out the counterfeits. It was a brilliant move, because when the real battle came, the Germans weren't ready; they had used up their ammunition on dummies.

Too many of us have made the same mistake. It's crazy how often Christians fight over things that aren't significant. We use up our ammunition fighting dummies, heatedly sparring over theological minutia, drawing abstract lines in the sand, obsessing over who's in and who's out, putting up barriers and walls around the kingdom of God. Meanwhile, the real enemy is taking ground. In Luke 9, one of Jesus' disciples smugly told him, "We saw someone driving out demons in your name and we tried to stop him, because he is not one of us" (v. 49). Two thousand years later, we haven't changed much, have we?

I love Jesus' response: "Do not stop him . . . for whoever is not against you is for you" (v. 50).

What a broad, beautiful, generous, hope-filled, gracious response.

How I pray for that kind of heart. It's been said:

In essentials, unity.
In non-essentials, liberty.
In all things, charity.

The heart of the gospel is love. And the heart of love is Jesus. If our theology isn't making us more loving, generous, and kind, then something is wrong with our theology. Maybe some of it needs to go. Maybe some of it needs to change. Or maybe we need to change.

Either way, doubt can expose what's defective and expendable in our faith. It has a purifying energy that challenges us to cut away the nonessentials while returning us to the essential One Thing.

>> <<

Of course, whenever you decide to throw something overboard, it can be excruciating. The word *decision* comes from the Latin root *cis* or *cid*. It literally means to "cut" or to "kill."[4] Because certainty feels so much better than mystery, when the basket goes, so does our sense of security. A part of us falls too.

It may be our wrong beliefs or ideas about God that need to go. Or, it may be something wrong in us.

Now, just to warn you, this point stings a bit, but I need to say it.

Sometimes, doubt can be a smoke screen for sin, or an excuse to live without moral boundaries. Sometimes we leverage doubt to justify our own brokenness. But if we're being real with ourselves and God, the issue may not be doubt at all, but something secretive and malignant. We blame God and watch as our faith in him slips away. But, in reality, it's only because we've allowed darkness in, and the tension with the light makes us uncomfortable.

The mind won't believe what the heart won't obey.

The agnostic Aldous Huxley, in his book *Ends and Means*, said he *chose* not to believe, "Because it delivered me from trying to find meaning and freed me to my own erotic passions."[5]

That's a tragic statement but at least he told the truth. When we doubt, we genuinely need to ask ourselves if it's coming from a place of sincere intellectual or emotional struggle, or if it's just a symptom of a disordered soul. A good litmus test is to ask what you hope the outcome will be. Do you want to draw closer to God through your doubt? Do you long for deeper, more intimate faith? Are you willing to pursue and open yourself up to truth, wherever it may lead? If not, it's possible there's sin behind the doubt that's gotten between you and him.

What's the solution? Let it go. Unless God is enough, nothing else ever will be. Jesus said that if your eye causes you to stumble, gouge it out; if your hand causes you to sin, cut it off (Matthew 5:29–30). Obviously, Jesus isn't being literal, or else we'd all be blind and handless! But he is being radical. He wants you to be free. He wants your faith to thrive. Sin is the distortion of the masterpiece God is painting in your life.

Don't sacrifice your tomorrow for the desires of today.

Remember the One Thing. Whatever you need to throw off the side, do it. It's worth it in the end.

» «

Let me share one more thing you may need to let go: doubt itself. I know that may be surprising to say, especially in a book where I've argued for vigorous engagement with doubt. But hear me out.

In *Life of Pi*, there is this marvelous line: "Doubt is useful for a while. . . . But we must move on. To choose doubt as a philosophy of life is akin to choosing immobility as a means of transportation."[6]

What this means is that some forms of doubt are so brazenly unhealthy, so self-serving and burdensome, that they no longer serve you but themselves. Like a controlling, codependent relationship, it consumes you, saps you of strength, and holds you back from your calling.

You either need to have a serious DTR or part ways.

I'm not talking about throwing your brain overboard just so you can believe. Nor am I talking about blind acceptance without looking at the facts. What I'm saying is that there are times when we have examined our doubt, prayed through it, explored it from every angle, and still it won't let us go.

Or maybe the real issue is that we won't let it go.

My mind races back to the story of Thomas. He said he wouldn't believe unless he put his hand in Jesus' side. He refused to commit without physical, tangible evidence. Jesus graciously appeared and invited him to touch his wounds. Thomas did, and his faith was reborn. But then Jesus said these words: "Because you have seen me, you have believed; blessed are those who have not seen and yet have believed" (John 20:29).

When Jesus said, "those who have not seen," he was talking about you and me. Unlike the early disciples, we haven't seen Jesus or touched his wounds. We weren't there when Jesus rose again. Of course, that's what makes believing so hard. We're trusting in a story that is two thousand years removed from our own.

A lot of people, understandably, have a hard time with that. "See?" they say. "Christianity is irrational. It's for people who don't think." Or "Faith has no basis in reality. I'll only believe something if I have 100 percent proof."

At first glance, that may sound reasonable. But if you look closer, is it really a sustainable way to live your life? One-hundred percent certainty about anything is impossible. Your plans aren't certain. Your next breath isn't certain. You can't even be certain of you.

Maybe, as some philosophers say, we're all just brains in a vat, the product of some vast, demented, cosmic experiment. Or maybe the universe is just a speck of dust on the eyelash of a very large and insecure Siberian hamster. Who knows? If you're waiting for unending clarity in life, chances are you'll never get married, have kids, pursue a career, or join a church. You'll just linger around the edges of possibility, straining your eyes in search of evidence and affirmation. And chances are, you'll be waiting for a very long time.

That means, when it comes to our struggles with faith and doubt, we have a vital choice to make: we can either remain in a permanent place of indecision, allowing our doubt to sabotage our faith, or we can choose to trust. The problem with indecision, however, is that there is limited space in the basket and limited time before it falls. Sooner or later we have to decide what matters most. We must choose our one thing.

But what about all the unanswered questions I have? What about my doubt? Like you, I also feel the sharp pangs of a restless faith. I get it. But here's what I'm learning: sometimes the most liberating words are *I don't know.* I don't know why parts of the Bible seem so violent. I don't know how to resolve certain scientific theories with my faith. I don't know why God allows suffering. I'm still confused by his silence. In this book I've tried to offer some steps toward resolution. But most of the time, the wall between confusion and clarity seems unbreachable. We should never abandon the quest to get through, though, nor do I believe that God wants us to. He relentlessly invites us deeper in.

But at the same time, he wants us to trust. Because, ultimately, what matters more than certainty is relationship. And sometimes, for the sake of relationship, we have to surrender our misgivings to bring love near. If certainty is the most important thing to you,

you'll discover it's jealous and unforgiving. You'll never fully settle because you'll never find what you're looking for. But if you value relationship, you'll experience intimacy. You can still pursue the unknown, but you won't do it alone. You'll still have doubt, but you'll also have love. And love always trusts. Always endures. And love lives in the hope that someday, somehow, all our tension, angst, worries, wonders, and doubts will be resolved.

Until then, move on. Decide what you need most in the basket.

If you choose Jesus, cling to him. Love him. Pursue him.

And if anything gets in the way. . .

Go ahead. Cut the basket. He'll get you home.

>> <<

A few months after my bizarre and hilarious conversation around the fire in Vanuatu, I had another unforgettable experience. A couple of miles away from the school where I taught, at the end of a long and dusty road, was a small hill overlooking the ocean. I often walked down that road for time alone (I'm a raging introvert), and I'd sit on the hill reading, thinking, and praying.

One day, my peaceful contemplation was interrupted by wild, high-pitched yells bursting out of the jungle. I looked over and saw about a dozen half-naked, spear-wielding, painted men running right at me. I froze. My mind raced. I had heard a few days before that there were parts of Vanuatu that had, until very recently, practiced cannibalism. I wondered grimly if that was how I was going to die. *Perhaps*, I thought, *I should give them the cold shoulder* (which is a terrible cannibal joke).

As they got closer, I realized, with huge relief, they weren't there to eat me but to have a spear-throwing contest.

I watched in awe as they each took turns hurling their personally crafted wooden spears off the side of the hill. Their aim was to see who could throw the farthest. Evidently, the winner would become a hero in their village. The stakes were high, and it was fascinating to see. I was amazed at how intricately designed the spears were, and even more amazed at how far they could throw them.

And then. . .

I don't know if it was curiosity or pride (most likely a mixture of both), but I asked if I could join the competition. They looked surprised.

One of them smiled. "Sure," he said. And he thrust his spear into my hand.

Now I was committed. They all watched me eagerly, bemused, as I fiddled awkwardly with the spear, trying to figure out where best to hold it. I then took a couple quick steps and, with everything in me, I hurled it down the hill.

Or so I thought.

In reality, it went about six feet, then twisted and flopped clumsily on the ground.

I couldn't believe it.

Immediately, they started laughing. Hysterically. It was the funniest thing they had ever seen. One of them led a chant: "He can't throw! He can't throw!" Another began to imitate my failed attempt, wildly throwing his hands around in the air. To my right, a man was literally rolling on the ground in laughter.

Humiliated, I ran toward the spear and tried again. And again. It's been said that insanity is doing the same thing over and over again and expecting different results. That was me on that lonely hill.

Finally, one of them felt sorry for me. He walked up, took the spear from my hands, and, with a smile, said, "You're terrible."

"I know." At least he was honest.

"Listen," he said.

I leaned in.

"Stop trying so hard. You can't force it. You're trying to make the spear fly. But that won't work."

He then pointed up. "You've got to let the wind carry it for you. Trust the wind. It's stronger than you."

He put the spear back in my hands. I tried again.

The spear went twice as far, which isn't saying much.

I never became the hero of the village that day. But I had learned a valuable lesson.

Sometimes the only way to fly is by letting go.

Conclusion

I'VE ALWAYS BEEN FASCINATED by last words. Whether it's the last words of a book, the closing remarks in a speech, or the final moments of a person's life, what's expressed at the end can speak volumes. The comedian W. C. Fields, when asked why he was reading the Bible on his deathbed, is reported to have said, "I'm looking for loopholes." Dominique Bouhours, the famous French grammarian, muttered, "I am about to, or I am going to, die. Either expression is correct." Steve Jobs's final words were, "Oh, wow!" What a perfect summary of his life.

Last words reveal so much!

According to the Gospels, Jesus' last words before ascending to heaven were, "Go and make disciples of all nations . . . I am with you always" (Matthew 28:19–20). Some last words are about summarizing life, but Jesus' last words were about inspiring a compelling vision for life. "Go." From that moment on, his disciples scattered into the world, and within a generation they turned it upside down (Acts 17:6).

What strikes me about that story, however, is not just the words Jesus said, but the people he said them to: "When they saw him, they worshiped him; but some doubted" (Matthew 28:17).

Wait. What?

Some doubted?

Keep in mind Jesus had just risen from the dead, and they had personally witnessed this historic event. They clung to his feet when he burst from the tomb after three days. They sat with him around a fire of coals as he cooked them fish for breakfast. They cautiously touched the wounds left by the iron Roman nails. Jesus' resurrection wasn't an idea they invented to give them purpose, a hallucination, or a way to manage grief. It was real. He was real. They could see him standing there.

But they still doubted.

It's fascinating that the authors of the New Testament decided to include that little detail, even though it could hurt their credibility. But what's even more fascinating is that Jesus wasn't upset.

He didn't rebuke the doubters. He didn't separate them from the believers. He didn't send out one group and leave the others behind.

No. Both doubters and believers were with him on the mountain. Both doubters and believers heard his gracious words. And both doubters and believers were dispatched to carry out his mission.

Like Jesus' first disciples, you have been called into a story that is larger than your own. Your life throbs with purpose. You were created to know and follow him. Your heart longs for this. And every one of us, worshippers and doubters, are invited to participate.

He calls the disciples whose faith never seems to waver. It's like they've always believed, humming Hillsong in their mothers' wombs, and haven't let up since. But he also calls the doubters. The confused, skeptical, restless, daring luchadors. Those with an unshakable ache for intimacy because they cannot stomach a faith that is not their own.

Jesus welcomes both. Both are called. Both are sent. Both are vital to the revolution he has begun.

And no matter where you are in your journey of faith, he calls you too.

Maybe you're far from home, and you don't know what or if you believe anymore. Or maybe you've moved past deconstruction and now you're exploring the terrain of doubt, engaging life's hardest questions. Or maybe you're on your way home. Your relationship with God is different than it was, but it's better somehow. Deeper. More alive.

Wherever you are, and whatever you think of God, endless possibility lies in front of you. Jesus' first recorded words to his disciples were, "Come, follow me," and his last words were essentially the same. Keep moving forward. Keep chasing after truth. The greatest danger is not that we lose our faith but that we settle for a mediocre version of it. Every day is an opportunity to ask, seek, knock. There is so much more to explore. So much more to learn. So much to soak in. There are rugged mountains to climb, challenges to overcome, vistas to take in, beauty to experience. A God to know.

You're just getting started.

And when your heart wavers, when your knees buckle, and when your faith fails, remember that you have this hope:

Jesus has the last word.

Acknowledgments

I AM BEYOND GRATEFUL for my wife, Elyssa. You encouraged this work, cheered me on as I wrote it, and worked tirelessly behind the scenes to help make it a reality. Even though you've heard these stories a thousand times, you patiently listened and gave input as I read them again (and again) to you. Thank you for being so supportive, loving, and kind.

I am also thankful for my daughter, Amelia. You inspire me in so many ways! You radiate so much joy and passion for life. I love you.

Thank you to my parents who showed me what deep faith looks like and what it means to follow Jesus when the sun goes dark.

Gerry Breshears, you have been such a formative, faithful presence in my life. Thank you for your willingness to plow through the unedited early drafts. Your wisdom was invaluable.

Also, Joshua Butler, your honesty, brilliance, taste in restaurants, and supportive feedback meant so much. Thank you!

Sal and Thalia Cesario, thank you so much for letting me retreat to your beautiful house in Bend to write this book. You've been unbelievably kind and generous.

Tim McDonald, Mike McDonald, Bob Goff, and Phil

Comer, for your prayers and encouragement. I love doing ministry with you!

Tom Baker, for your photography and videography, and most importantly, friendship.

Scott Bakken, for giving me the photo you took in Israel that became the cover of this book. You're insanely gifted, and I'm in awe of your creative genius!

A huge thank you to Bill Jensen, Jessica Wong, and the Nelson Books team. This book wouldn't exist without you.

Finally, I want to thank Westside: A Jesus Church, its staff, and elders. It is such an honor to serve alongside you and to participate in the story that God is writing. Thank you for your love, support, and the endless grace you've shown to my family.

Notes

CHAPTER 1: KNOWING WE DON'T KNOW

1. Jean-Jacques Rousseau, *Fundamental Political Writings* (Ontario, Canada: Broadview Press, 2018), 51.

2. John Milton, *Paradise Lost* (London: John Bumpus, 1821), 103.

3. Ronald Rolheiser, *The Holy Longing: The Search for a Christian Spirituality* (New York: Random House, 2014), 9.

4. "Google Search Statistics," Internet Live Stats, accessed May 19, 2018, http://www.internetlivestats.com/google-search-statistics/.

5. Frederick Buechner, *Beyond Words: Daily Readings in the ABC's of Faith* (New York: Harper Collins, 2004), 85.

6. David E. Rowe and Robert Schulmann, eds., *Einstein on Politics* (Princeton, NJ: Princeton University Press, 2007), 229.

CHAPTER 2: BETWEEN TWO WORLDS

1. Dwight Garner, "John Updike," Salon, February 24, 1999, https://www.salon.com/1999/02/24/updike_4/.

2. H. G. Wells, *The Country of the Blind and Other Science-Fiction Stories*, ed. Martin Gardner (Mineola, NY: Dover Publications, 2011).

3. Oxford English Dictionary, s.v. "doubt," accessed May 21, 2018, https://en.oxforddictionaries.com/definition/doubt.

4. Os Guinness, *God in the Dark: The Assurance of Faith Beyond a Shadow of Doubt* (Wheaton, IL: Crossway, 1996), 23.

5. Guinness, 23.

6. James K. A. Smith, *How (Not) to Be Secular: Reading Charles Taylor* (Grand Rapids, MI: Wm. B. Eerdmans, 2014), 4.

7. Dan Merica, "Pew Survey: Doubt of God Growing Quickly Among Millennials," *CNN Belief Blog*, June 12, 2012, http://religion.blogs.cnn.com/2012/06/12/pew-survey-doubt-of-god-growing-quickly-among-millennials/.

8. "Two-Thirds of Christians Face Doubt," Barna, July 25, 2017, https://www.barna.com/research/two-thirds-christians-face-doubt/.

9. Jonathan Morrow, "Why Generation Z Is Less Christian Than Ever—and Why That's Good News," Fox News, March 11, 2018, http://www.foxnews.com/opinion/2018/03/11/why-generation-z-is-less-christian-than-ever-and-why-thats-good-news.html.

10. Wikiquote, s.v. "Jean-Paul Sartre," last modified April 22, 2018, https://en.wikiquote.org/wiki/Jean-Paul_Sartre.

11. The author Ben Young uses the metaphor of ice to describe doubt. Doubt is slippery, but it also has the potential to move us closer to God or away. Ben Young, *Room for Doubt: How Uncertainty Can Deepen Your Faith* (Colorado Springs: David C. Cook, 2017), kindle loc. 314.

12. Dominique Lapierre, "'The Poor Must Be Loved' Her Message Was Forged in a Caldron of Misery," *The Spokesman-Review*, September 6, 1997, http://www.spokesman.com/stories/1997/sep/06/the-poor-must-be-loved-her-message-was-forged-in/.

13. Mother Teresa, *Mother Teresa: Come Be My Light: The Private Writings of the Saint of Calcutta*, ed. Brian Kolodiejchuk (New York: Crown Publishing Group, 2007), 187.

14. "Mother Teresa of Calcutta—Quotes & Stories," Crossroads Initiative, accessed May 21, 2018, https://www.crossroadsinitiative.com/saints/quotes-from-blessed-mother-teresa-of-calcutta/.

15. Søren Kierkegaard, *Provocations: Spiritual Writings of Kierkegaard* (Walden, NY: Plough Publishing House, 2002), 104.

16. Quoted in John Ortberg, *Who Is This Man? Study Guide: The Unpredictable Impact of the Inescapable Jesus* (Grand Rapids, MI: Zondervan, 2012), 43.

17. Friedrich Nietzsche, *Complete Works of Friedrich Nietzsche* (UK: Delphi Classics, 2015), loc. 40045, Kindle.
18. Nietzsche, loc. 34025–26, Kindle.
19. Nietzsche, loc. 17501–04, Kindle.
20. William Shakespeare, *Hamlet*, act 3, scene 2, line 254.
21. D. Martyn Lloyd-Jones, *Spiritual Depression: Its Causes and Its Cure* (Grand Rapids, MI: Eerdmans, 1965), 154.

CHAPTER 3: WHEN THE SUN GOES DARK

1. Zoe Schlanger, "Witnessing an Eclipse Is So Overwhelming It Has Created a Global Community of 'Addicts,'" Quartz, August 12, 2017, https://qz.com/1051179/the-thrill-of-an-eclipse-is-so-overwhelming-that-its-turned-hundreds-of-people-into-addicts/.
2. Walter Brueggemann, *Spirituality of the Psalms* (Minneapolis, MN: Augsburg Fortress, 2002), 16–57.
3. Hyman Gerson Enelow, *The Varied Beauty of the Psalms* (New York: Bloch Publishing Company, 1917), 65.
4. Lettie Ransley, "A Grief Observed by CS Lewis—Review," *The Guardian*, August 11, 2013, https://www.theguardian.com/books/2013/aug/11/grief-observed-cs-lewis-review.
5. Friedrich Nietzsche, *The Gay Science* (New York: Random House, 1974), 181.
6. Gregory A. Boyd, *Benefit of the Doubt: Breaking the Idol of Certainty* (Grand Rapids, MI: Baker Books, 2013), 44.
7. Christopher G. Ellison et al., "Religious Doubts and Sleep Quality: Findings from a Nationwide Study of Presbyterians," *Review of Religious Research* 53, no. 2 (November 2011): 119–36, https://www.ncbi.nlm.nih.gov/pmc/articles/PMC3448782/.
8. Quoted in Gregory Boyd, *Benefit of the Doubt: Breaking the Idol of Certainty* (Grand Rapids, MI: Baker Books), 23.
9. Saint Augustine, *The Confessions* (New York: New City Press, 1997), 262.

CHAPTER 4: I SEE STARS

1. "Bishops Ridley and Latimer Burned," Christianity.com, April 28, 2010, https://www.christianity.com/church/church-history /timeline/1501–1600/bishops-ridley-and-latimer-burned-11629990 .html.

2. Ian Sample, "Stephen Hawking: 'There Is No Heaven; It's a Fairy Story,'" *The Guardian*, May 15, 2011, https://www.theguardian.com/science/2011/may/15 /stephen-hawking-interview-there-is-no-heaven.

3. Bob Seidensticker, "John Lennox Responds to Stephen Hawking," *Cross Examined* (blog), August 29, 2011, http://www.patheos.com/blogs/crossexamined/2011/08 /john-lennox-responds-to-stephen-hawking/.

4. Gary Habermas, *The Thomas Factor: Using Your Doubts to Draw Closer to God* (Nashville, TN: Broadman & Holman, 1999).

5. Richard Dawkins, *River Out of Eden* (New York: Basic Books, 1995), 133.

6. John Gray, *Straw Dogs: Thoughts on Humans and Other Animals* (New York: Farrar, Straus and Giroux, 2003), 26.

7. Gray, *Straw Dogs*, xii.

8. Fyodor Dostoevsky, *The Brothers Karamazov* (New York: Farrar, Straus and Giroux, 2002).

9. "Karl Barth Quotes," Goodreads, accessed May 21, 2018, https://www.goodreads.com /quotes/338144-i-haven-t-even-read-everything-i-wrote.

10. Christopher J. H. Wright, *The God I Don't Understand: Reflections on Tough Questions of Faith* (Grand Rapids, MI: Zondervan, 2008), 15–16.

11. Thomas Nagel, *The Last Word* (New York: Oxford University Press, 1997), 130.

12. Dale Carnegie, *How to Stop Worrying and Start Living: Time-Tested Methods for Conquering Worry* (New York: Simon and Schuster, 1984), 139.

13. Blaise Pascal, *Pascal's Pensees* (New York: Dutton and Co., 1958), 67.

14. Skye Jethani, *Futureville: Discover Your Purpose for Today by Reimagining Tomorrow* (Nashville, TN: Thomas Nelson, 2014), Kindle edition 147–148.

CHAPTER 5: CAN I TRUST THE BIBLE?

1. Friedrich Paulsen, *Immanuel Kant, His Life and Doctrine*, trans. J. E. Creighton and Albert Lefevre (New York: Charles Scribner's Sons, 1902), 48.

2. "10 Different Ways to Look at Iconic Black Pioneers," PBS.org, accessed May 23, 2018, http://www.pbs.org/black-culture /explore/10-new-ways-to-look-at-black-pioneers/#.WtuPEyOZNTY.

3. Quoted in Neil Cole, *Organic Church: Growing Faith Where Life Happens* (San Francisco: Jossey-Bass, 2005), 61.

4. Vishal Mangalwadi, *The Book That Made Your World: How the Bible Created the Soul of Western Civilization* (Nashville, TN: Thomas Nelson, 2011).

5. Lydia Saad, "Record Few Americans Believe Bible Is Literal Word of God," Gallup.org, May 15, 2017, http://news.gallup.com/poll /210704/record-few-americans-believe-bible-literal-word-god.aspx.

6. Christopher Ingraham, "The Long, Steady Decline of Literary Reading," *The Washington Post*, September 7, 2016, https://www .washingtonpost.com/news/wonk/wp/2016/09/07/the-long-steady -decline-of-literary-reading/?utm_term=.680458f50ab0.

7. Stephen Prothero, *Religious Literacy: What Every American Needs to Know—And Doesn't* (New York: HarperCollins, 2007), 6.

8. "Mark Twain Quotes," Goodreads, accessed May 23, 2018, https://www.goodreads.com/quotes/85747-it-ain-t-the-parts -of-the-bible-that-i-can-t.

9. Craig L. Blomberg, *Can We Still Believe the Bible?: An Evangelical Engagement with Contemporary Questions* (Grand Rapids, MI: Brazos Press, 2014), 29.

10. Quoted in Josh McDowell and Bill Wilson, *Evidence for the Historical Jesus: A Compelling Case for His Life and His Claims* (Eugene, OR: Harvest House Publishers, 1993), 113.

11. E. Randolph Richards, *Misreading Scripture with Western Eyes: Removing Cultural Blinders to Better Understand the Bible* (Downers Grove, IL: InterVarsity, 2012), 11.

12. Eugene H. Peterson, *Eat This Book: A Conversation in the Art of Spiritual Reading* (Grand Rapids, MI: Wm. B. Eerdmans, 2006), 11.

13. Philip Yancey, *The Bible Jesus Read* (Grand Rapids, MI: Zondervan, 1999), 24–25.

CHAPTER 6: IS SCIENCE THE ENEMY OF FAITH?

1. *The Simpsons*, season 9, episode 8, "Lisa the Skeptic," directed by Neil Affleck, written by David X. Cohen and Matt Selman, aired November 23, 1997, on Fox, https://www.amazon.com /The-Simpsons-Season-9/dp/B071FRX2DK/.

2. Andrew Dickson White, *A History of the Warfare of Science with Theology in Christendom* (New York: D. Appleton and Company, 1901), ix.

3. Quoted in R. J. Berry, *God and Evolution: Creation, Evolution and the Bible* (Vancouver: Regent College Publishing, 2001), 13.

4. Cary Funk and Becka Alper, "Religion and Science," Pew Research Center, October 22, 2015, http://www.pewinternet.org/2015/10/22 /science-and-religion/.

5. Alvin Plantinga, *Where the Conflict Really Lies: Science, Religion, and Naturalism* (New York: Oxford University Press, 2011), 5.

6. Jerry A. Coyne, *Faith Versus Fact: Why Science and Religion Are Incompatible* (New York: Penguin Publishing, 2015), xvi.

7. Jonathan Sacks, *The Great Partnership: Science, Religion, and the Search for Meaning* (New York: Schocken Books, 2011), 12.

8. Ricky Gervais, "Why I Do Not Believe in a God," December 22, 2010, *Wall Street Journal*, https://www.wsj.com/articles/SB1000142 4052748703886690457603164010215415.

9. Sacks, *The Great Partnership*, 6–7.

10. William Shakespeare, *Hamlet*, act 1, scene 5, lines 187–88.

11. Plantinga, *Where the Conflict Really Lies*.

12. Galileo Galilei, "Letter to the Grand Duchess Christine of Tuscany (1615)," https://web.stanford.edu/~jsabol/certainty/readings /Galileo-LetterDuchessChristina.pdf.

13. "Scientists and Belief," Pew Research Center, November 5, 2009, http://www.pewforum.org/2009/11/05/scientists-and-belief/.

14. Carol Kuruvilla, "12 Famous Scientists on the Possibility of God," HuffPost, April 11, 2017, https://www.huffingtonpost .com/entry/12-famous-scientists-on-the-possibility-of-god _us_56afa292e4b057d7d7c7a1e5.

15. Jonathan Sacks, "The Necessity of Asking Questions," *The Office of Rabbi Sacks* (blog), January 30, 2017, http://rabbisacks.org /necessity-asking-questions-bo-5777/.

16. James Hannam, *God's Philosophers: How the Medieval World Laid the Foundations of Modern Science* (London: Icon Books, 2009), 6.

17. St. Augustine, *The Literal Meaning of Genesis*, vol. 1, trans. and annot. John Hammond Taylor (New York: Newman Press, 1982), 42–43.

18. John Lennox, *God's Undertaker: Has Science Buried God?* (Oxford: Lion Hudson, 2007), 44.

CHAPTER 7: WHY IS THE WORLD SO BROKEN?

1. Jonathan Sacks, *The Great Partnership: Science, Religion, and the Search for Meaning* (New York: Schocken Books, 2011), 233–34.

2. "Irving Greenberg (1933-)," Jewish Virtual Library, accessed May 23, 2018, http://www.jewishvirtuallibrary.org /irving-greenberg.

3. Søren Kierkegaard, *Either/Or: A Fragment of Life* (New York: Penguin Books, 1992), 1.

4. Quoted in Christopher Southgate, *The Groaning of Creation: God, Evolution, and the Problem of Evil* (Louisville, KY: Westminster John Knox Press, 2008), 33.

5. Henri Blocher, *Evil and the Cross: An Analytical Look at the Problem of Pain* (Grand Rapids, MI: Kregel Publications, 1994), 133.

6. Quoted in Nick Vujicic, *Be the Hands and Feet: Living Out God's Love for All His Children* (New York: WaterBrook, 2018), 1. Punctuation changed for emphasis.

7. A similar idea is found in the poem "The Master Weaver's Plan." Holocaust survivor, Corrie ten Boom, used the poem to speak of God's redemption, https://www.challies.com/articles /gods-tapestry/.

8. Fyodor Dostoevsky, *The Brothers Karamazov* (Andronum, CreateSpace, 2018), 84.

CHAPTER 8: WHY IS GOD SILENT?

1. Shusaku Endo, *Silence*, trans. William Johnston (New York: Picador, 1969), 64.

2. Michael Rea, *Evil and the Hiddenness of God* (Stamford, CT: Cengage Learning, 2015), 163.

3. St. John of the Cross, *The Spiritual Canticle*, Catholic Treasury, accessed May 23, 2018, http://www.catholictreasury.info/books /spiritual_canticle/cn_4.php.

4. Lisa Eadicicco, "Americans Check Their Phones 8 Billion Times a Day," *TIME*, December 15, 2015, http://time.com/4147614 /smartphone-usage-us-2015/.

5. Maya Angelou, *I Know Why the Caged Bird Sings* (New York: Random House, 1969), 11.

6. *The Oxford Book of Mystical Verse*, chosen by D.H.S. Nicholson and A.H.E. Lee (Oxford: The Clarendon Press, 1917), 152.

7. Todd B. Bates, "Deep Roots in Plants Driven by Soil Hydrology," Rutgers Today, September 18, 2017, https://news.rutgers .edu/deep-roots-plants-driven-soil-hydrology/20170915# .Wh9PdraZPOQ.

8. Søren Kierkegaard, *Parables of Kierkegaard* (Princeton, NJ: Princeton University Press, 1989), 42.

9. Mother Teresa, *In the Heart of the World: Thoughts, Stories, and Prayers* (Novato, CA: New World Library, 1997), 19.

10. C. S. Lewis, *Till We Have Faces: A Myth Retold* Pte LTd 1956

CHAPTER 9: THE LUCHADOR

1. Jonathan Sacks, *The Great Partnership: Science, Religion, and the Search for Meaning* (New York: Schocken Books, 2011), 97.

2. Warren Wiersbe, *The Wiersbe Bible Commentary: Old Testament* (Colorado Springs: David C. Cook, 2007), 444.

3. Kallistos Ware, *The Orthodox Way* (Crestwood, NY: St. Vladimir's Seminary Press, 1979), 16.

4. Quoted in John Ortberg, *Faith and Doubt* (Grand Rapids, MI: Zondervan, 2008), 24.

5. Quoted in: Charles Swindoll, *The Inspirational Writings* (New York: BBS Publishing Corporation, 1994), 21.

6. Vincent J. Donovan, *Christianity Rediscovered* (Maryknoll, NY: Orbis Books, 1978).

7. Peter Kreeft, *Prayer for Beginners* (San Francisco: Ignatius Press, 2000), 35.

8. Charles Taylor, *A Secular Age* (Cambridge, MA: Harvard University Press, 2007), 38.

9. Donovan, *Christianity Rediscovered*, 48.

CHAPTER 10: BE THE ANSWER

1. Eugene H. Peterson, *A Long Obedience in the Same Direction: Discipleship in an Instant Society* (Downers Grove, IL: InterVarsity Press, 2000).

2. Richard Dawkins, *The God Delusion* (New York: Houghton Mifflin, 2006), 347.

3. Keith Ferdinando, "Jesus, the Theological Educator," *Themelios* 38, no. 3, ed. D. A. Carson (November 2013): 366, https://www.thegospelcoalition.org/article/themelios-38–3/.

4. Alexander Pope, *An Essay on Criticism*, public domain.

5. Eugene H. Peterson, *First and Second Samuel* (Louisville, KY: Westminster Knox Press, 1999), 144.

6. Larry D. Rosen, "Welcome to the iGeneration!" *Psychology Today*, March 27, 2010, https://www.psychologytoday.com/blog/rewired-the-psychology-technology/201003/welcome-the-igeneration.

7. David Kinnaman, *You Lost Me: Why Young Christians Are Leaving Church . . . and Rethinking Faith* (Grand Rapids, MI: Baker Books, 2011), 11.

8. Anne Lamott, *Hallelujah Anyway: Rediscovering Mercy* (New York: Riverhead Books, 2017), 50.

9. Henri J. M. Nouwen, *The Wounded Healer: Ministry in Contemporary Society* (New York: Doubleday, 1979).

10. "Francis of Assisi Quotes," Goodreads, accessed May 23, 2018, https://www.goodreads.com/quotes/400106-we-have-been-called-to -heal-wounds-to-unite-what.

11. "Mother Teresa of Calcutta—Quotes & Stories," Crossroads Initiative, accessed May 23, 2018, https://www.crossroadsinitiative .com/saints/quotes-from-blessed-mother-teresa-of-calcutta/.

12. Dargan Thompson, "11 Essential Bonhoeffer Quotes," *Relevant Magazine*, April 8, 2016, https://relevantmagazine.com/culture /books/12-essential-bonhoeffer-quotes.

13. A. W. Tozer, *This World: Playground or Battleground?* (Chicago: Moody Publishers, 1989), Kindle edition, loc 103–118.

CHAPTER 11: BALLOONS AND SPEARS

1. Jules Verne, *The Mysterious Island* (Hertfordshire: Wordsworth Editions Limited, 2010), 21.

2. Verne, *The Mysterious Island*, 25.

3. Søren Kierkegaard, *Provocations: Spiritual Writings of Kierkegaard* (Walden, NY: Plough Publishing House, 2002), 33.

4. Greg McKeown, *Essentialism: The Disciplined Pursuit of Less* (New York: Crown Business, 2014), 159.

5. Aldous Huxley, *Ends and Means: An Inquiry into the Nature of Ideals* (London: Chatt & Windus, 1946), 310.

6. Yann Martel, *Life of Pi* (Orlando, FL: Harcourt Books, 2001), 28.

About the Author

DOMINIC DONE is lead pastor of Westside: A Jesus Church in Portland, Oregon. He has a master's in theology from the University of Oxford and a master's in religion from Liberty University. He previously served as a pastor in North Carolina and Hawaii. He has also taught English for companies in Europe, lectured in theology and history at various Christian colleges, worked as a radio DJ, and lived as a missionary in Vanuatu and Mexico. Dominic is married to his wife, Elyssa, has a daughter named Amelia, and a fuzzy goldendoodle, Bella. You can connect with Dominic online at dominicdone.com, Facebook, or Instagram and Twitter @dominicdone.